CHILDREN'S ENCYCLOPEDIA OF CHEMISTRY

Janet Bingham

ARCTURUS

Picture Credits:
Every attempt has been made to clear copyright. Should there be any inadvertent omission, please apply to the publisher for rectification.

Key: b–bottom, t–top, c–center, l–left, r–right

Alamy Stock Photo: 10cl (PA Images), 18bl (Pictorial Press Ltd), 28–29c (Rings and jewelery), 32–33c (imageBROKER), 34c (Robert Brook/ Science Photo Library), 40tl (Dorling Kindersley Ltd), 42–43 (H. Mark Weidman Photography), 52–53c (RooM the Agency), 53br (Historic Images), 68–69c (DonSmith), 101tl (Science History Images), 101br (Archive PL), 124tr (Mopic); **Cornell University:** 84tl; **Getty Images:** 24–25c (2011 Sara Dawn Johnson), 36–37c (Image Source), 76bl (denisk0); **NASA:** 80–81c; **Nature Picture Library:** 102–102 (Nick Upton); **Science History Institute:** 110bl; **Science Photo Library:** 5tl (Andrew Lambert Photography), 5c (Robert Brook), 14cl (NOBEASTSOFIERCE), 18–19c (ANDREW LAMBERT PHOTOGRAPHY), 23br (Universal History Archive / UIG), 35tr (TOM HOLLYMAN), 45bc (EYE OF SCIENCE), 48–49c & 78br (MARTYN F. CHILLMAID), 49tr (Turtle Rock Scientific), 48br (SCIENCE SOURCE), 50–51c (Michael Penev/US DEPARTMENT OF ENERGY), 54cl (Alexandre Dotta/Science Source), 64–65c (SAKKMESTERKE), 68bl (PEGGY GREB / US DEPARTMENT OF AGRICULTURE), 73t, 74br, 75br, 76–77c, 84br SCIENCE PHOTO LIBRARY), 118cl, 118bl (Hagley Museum and Archive); **Shutterstock:** 1 (Rattiya Thongdumhyu) 6–7c (New Africa), 6cl (Albertm24), 6br (Lilkin), 7br (fortton), 8–9c (kmls), 9tr (Prostock-studio), 9cr (Kostsov), 10–11c (YouraPechkin), 10b (Net Vector), 11tr (Hecos), 12–13c (VasiliyBudarin), 12tr (Andy Dean Photography), 12bl (successo images), 13br (petrroudny43), 14–15c (Peter Mayer 67), 15tl (Curioso.Photography), 16–17c (Engineer studio), 16br (Chaleephoto), 17br (Chaleephoto), 19tr (trgrowth), 20–21c Halfpoint, 20br (Maria Symchych), 21br (nguyen thi phuong dieu), 20cl (Stephen Mcsweeny), 21tr (Incomible), 22–23c (VH-studio), 22cr (Stivog), 22bl (maradon 333), 24bl (pio3), 25br (Baiphai Bamboo), 26–27c (Bedrin), 26bl (Atlantist Studio), 26tr (anchalee thaweeboon), 27tr (zizou7), 28cl (Charles Shapiro), 28br, 30–31c (Idutko), 30cl (peterschreiber.media), 31tl (Kedar Vision), 31bc (MarcelClemens), 31c (Sansanorth), 32bl (zizou7), 32tl (LoopAll), 34–35c (New Africa), 34b (Lookiepix), 36tl (Jo Sam Re), 36c (Jo Sam Re), 37tr (IT Tech Science), 38–39c (Robert Kneschke), 38c (Sergey Merkulov), 39tl (ggw), 40–41c (William Perugini), 41tr (ANATOLY Foto), 42cr (Mark Agnor), 42bc (WillemijnB), 43cr (Sokor Space, 44–45c (sebra), 44cl (Zigres), 45tr (Ulianenko Dmitrii), 46–47c (2DAssets), 46–47c (Art Stocker), 47br (ElenaTlt), 48cl (2DAssets), 48bl (trgrowth), 50cr (Douglas Cliff), 50bl (Evgeniyqw), 52cr (2DAssets), 52cr (trgrowth), 52bl (YARUNIV Studio), 53tr (Nataliia Budianska), 54–55c (Max Topchii), 55tl (New Africa), 55bc (Kitch Bain), 54bl (StudioMolekuul), 56–57c (Ivan Kurmyshov), 56c (Tawansak), 57tl (Roman Zaiets), 57bl (Feng Yu), 58–59c (Tina Gutierrez), 58tr (Jo Sam Re), 60–61 (Pozdeyev Vitaly), 60c (Sergey Merkulov), 61bc (Ake13bk), 62c (SritanaN), 62cl (Adisak Riwkratok), 63tc (Ali DM), 64l (buteo), 65bl (Egoreichenkov Evgenii), 65cr (OSweetNature), 66–67c (Ground Picture), 66tr (Tricky_Shark), 67tr (Ann Bulashenko), 68cr (zcxes), 70–71c (M. Schauer), 70c (elena moiseeva), 71ct (Radu Razvan), 71bl (Alexander Girich), 72–73c (New Africa), 72cr (chromatos), 72bl (Biology Education), 74–75c (Rafya Thongdumhyu), 74–75c (Inkoly), 74cl (Bjoern Wylezich), 76cl (Steve Cymro), 77tr (i viewfinder), 78–79c (Guitar photographer), 78tr (Nandalal Sarkar), 79tr (Rabbitmindphoto), 80cl (fencifd), 80br (N_CA), 81tr (Ajamal), 82–83c (S.Borisov), 82tr (TarTla), 82c (MoFarouk), 83bc (Cergios), 84–85c (Sergei Drozd), 86–87c (DeepSkyTX), 86cr (OSweetNature), 87br (Ad_hominem), 88–89c (DoJed YeT), 88cr (Photoongraphy), 88bl (VectorMine), 90–91c (Francesco ConT), 90c (VectorMine), 91cr (Vladimir Arndt), 92–93c (Dragos AsaWei), 92tr (Merkushev Vasiliy), 92tr (Kichigin), 93b (Maleo), 94–95c (Vitaliy Karimov), 94cr (GraphicsRF.com), 94bl (Peter Gudella), 96–97c (Melissa Burovac), 96cl (Seqoya), 96cr (VectorMine), 98–99c (TinaSova20), 98cr (petrroudny43), 98bl (Dark Moon Pictures), 100–101c (hutch photography), 100cr (DKN0049), 102bl (ju_see), 103bl (LillieGraphie), 103tr (popcorn–arts), 104–105c (winnond), 104br (Beautiful landscape), 105tl (ShadeDesign), 105br (Sandy Storm), 106–107c (ifong), 106tr (Dragana Goric), 106br (Boonchuay1970), 106cl (VaLiza), 108–109c (santypan), 108tr (Soho A Studio), 108bl (Suzuki Leo), 109b (leungchopan), 109tr (Se_vector), 110–111c (SofikoS), 110cl (Oleksiy Mark), 111br (MIA Studio); **University of Illinois Archives:** 62br; **Welcome Collection:** 37br, 51tr, 59tr, 95tr; **Wikimedia Commons:** 7tr, 8 br, 11br, 14br, 17tr, 25tr, 27br, 29tr, 30b (MRC Laboratory of Molecular Biology), 32br, 38br, 40br (Harvard University), 43br, 44br, 47tr, 56br, 60bl, 60br, 65tr, 66br (Science History Institute), 69 br (Letizia Mancino Cremer), 70br, 73br (Science History Institute), 79br (Huangdan2060), 81br, 82br, 85tr (University of Bristol), 87tr (Smithsonian Institution), 89br, 90br, 92br, 97br, 97tr, 107tr (CrutchDerm2014).

All cover images are **Shutterstock**: back cover (Guitar photographer), front cover main image (Gorodenkoff), front cover insets l–r (Helen J Davies), (Yurchanka Siarhei), (Elisa Manzati), (Romolo Tavani), (Sashkin).

ARCTURUS

This edition published in 2023 by Arcturus Publishing Limited
26/27 Bickels Yard, 151–153 Bermondsey Street,
London SE1 3HA

Author: Janet Bingham
Editors: Felicity Forster, Becca Clunes, Lydia Halliday
Designer: Lorraine Inglis
Picture research: Lorraine Inglis and Paul Futcher

ISBN: 978-1-3988-2576-5
CH010104US
Supplier 29, Date 0623, PI 00003234

Printed in China

CONTENTS

Introduction

Chemistry is the science of stuff. It investigates everything there is to know about different substances—whether they are natural, like rocks and water, or made by humans, such as plastics. Chemistry also investigates substances in living things, including the human body. No matter where a substance is found, it will always follow scientific rules.

Everything, Everywhere

It is easy to forget how much we rely on different materials each day. There are many millions of substances for chemists to study in different ways.

Atoms are too small to see, but they are made up of even smaller particles inside.

Atoms and Elements

Everything in the Universe is made from just 118 substances, called elements. Elements can combine to form substances with different properties. To understand elements, chemists study the tiny building blocks that make them up: atoms.

Transformations

One of the fascinating things about chemistry is how substances can change completely, like iron turning to rust or salt dissolving into water. Chemists have figured out how this happens.

Many of our everyday materials—like ice cream—are mixtures.

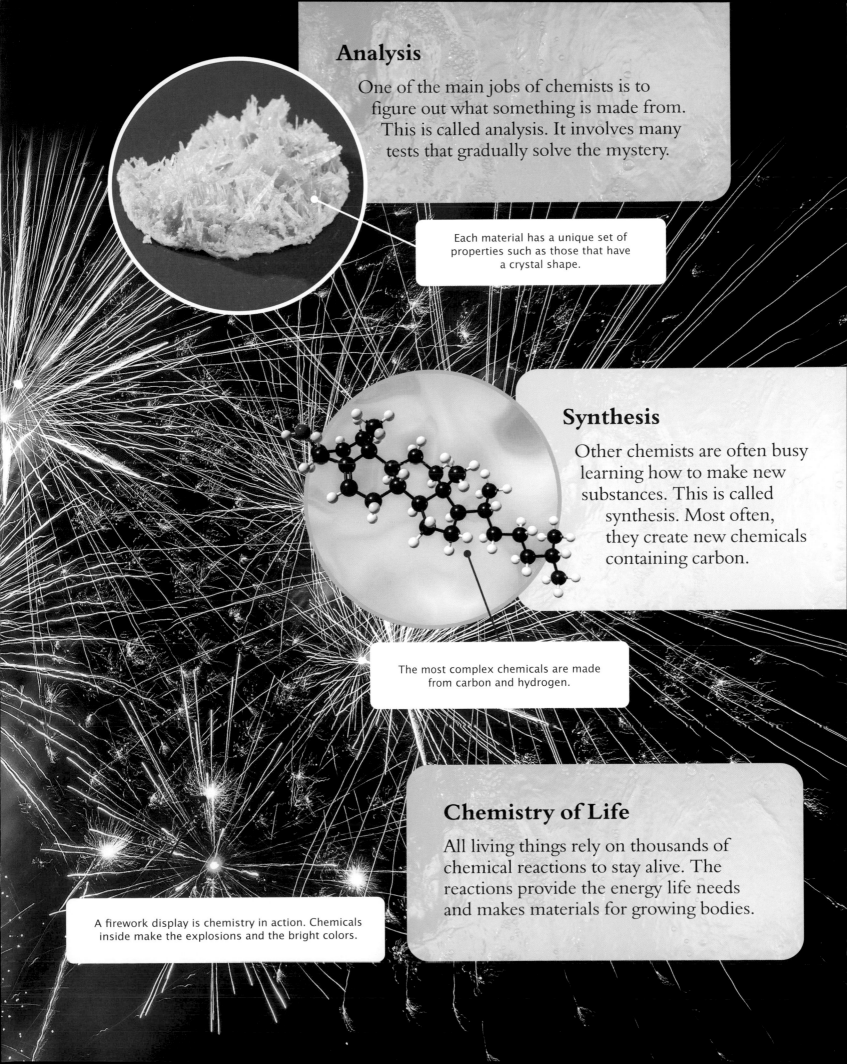

Analysis

One of the main jobs of chemists is to figure out what something is made from. This is called analysis. It involves many tests that gradually solve the mystery.

Each material has a unique set of properties such as those that have a crystal shape.

Synthesis

Other chemists are often busy learning how to make new substances. This is called synthesis. Most often, they create new chemicals containing carbon.

The most complex chemicals are made from carbon and hydrogen.

Chemistry of Life

All living things rely on thousands of chemical reactions to stay alive. The reactions provide the energy life needs and makes materials for growing bodies.

A firework display is chemistry in action. Chemicals inside make the explosions and the bright colors.

States of Matter

Matter is any substance that takes up space. It exists in three forms ("states" or "phases"), which are solids, liquids, and gases. All substances are in one of these three states at any time.

The sea is a liquid. It will take the shape of a bucket, but it will not expand to fill it.

Properties

Solids, liquids, and gases have different properties—they behave differently. You can hold a solid, and it won't change shape. Liquids run through your fingers, while gases can't be picked up at all. Scientists call both liquids and gases "fluids" because they flow and change shape to fit their containers. Shape and flow are properties of matter. Other properties are mass (the amount of matter), volume (the space it fills), density (heaviness), and compressibility (squashiness).

Oil floats on water because water is denser (heavier) than oil. Honey is denser than water. You can stack liquids of different densities in a jar, like this.

A pump compresses (squashes) air into a container. Gases have no definite volume, and they can be compressed. Solids and liquids are not easily compressed.

Properties of Mass, Volume, and Density

Solids and liquids have a definite volume and density, and these don't change, even when a liquid flows into a container. But when gases flow, they expand. The gas in a balloon becomes the shape of the balloon, and as more air is blown in, more pressure is put on the surface. If the balloon pops, the escaping gas flows out into the air, the mass of gas spreads out, and its volume and density change.

Maria the Alchemist was one of the first early scientists, or alchemists. She was already a historical figure by the fourth century when Zosimos of Panopolis quoted her work and described her as a "sage" (wise person). We think Maria invented some pieces of chemical apparatus, including the double-boiler for heating things gently. This was given the name "bain-marie" after Maria centuries later.

The air in an inflatable ball is a gas. When air is blown into the ball, it expands (spreads out) to fill the space.

Sand is a solid. It flows into a bucket, but importantly the size and shape of each tiny, individual grain of sand is solid and does not change.

Solids usually have a higher density than liquids, so they sink. But liquids are usually denser than gases, so solids that contain air will float.

A spade is a solid. Its shape and size don't change, unless it gets bent or broken.

DID YOU KNOW? Atmospheric pressure—the heaviness of air surrounding Earth—decreases with height. The change in pressure makes your ears pop in a plane.

Particle Theory

Solids, liquids, and gases behave differently. Solids have a shape, liquids flow, and gases escape in all directions. You can understand why, if you think of materials as made up of tiny, invisible balls, or particles. The particles' arrangement affects their properties (how they act). This is the particle theory of matter.

Solids and Liquids

In a solid, the particles are held tightly. They can't move around or change places. This gives the solid a definite shape and volume. It also makes it very dense (heavy) and hard to compress (squash). In liquids, the particles are held quite closely together, so liquids have a definite volume and are quite dense and hard to compress. But their particles are not neatly arranged. They can tumble past each other, so the liquid flows and changes shape.

Balls inside a ball pit are like the particles in a liquid. They are kept together, but they can move past each other. They flow to fit the shape of the ball pit.

Each ball is made of plastic. Plastic is a solid, so its particles are packed together, giving the ball a definite shape and size.

HALL OF FAME:
John Dalton
1766–1844

Dalton developed the idea of atomic theory. Other chemists wrongly believed that all particles (atoms) were alike. Dalton argued that the atoms of each element (the simplest chemicals) are alike, but that atoms of different elements are different. He also understood that when chemicals react, atoms rearrange into different compounds.

Gases and Diffusion

Gas particles are scattered and held together loosely. The wide spaces between them make the gas light and easy to compress. The particles have lots of energy to move around and spread out. This spreading is called diffusion. Gases have no definite volume. Their particles will diffuse until the gas has filled all the space it can, so a gas in a container will take on the shape of the container.

Cooking smells move through the house by diffusion. The delicious-smelling gas particles move freely through the air until they reach your nose!

Neatly stacked balls are like the particles in a solid. Each particle is held in place, and the substance has a definite shape and volume.

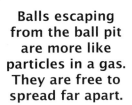

Balls escaping from the ball pit are more like particles in a gas. They are free to spread far apart.

DID YOU KNOW? Your body contains around 7 octillion atoms—that's 7,000,000,000,000,000,000,000,000,000!

9

Changing States

All materials are in one of the states of matter (solid, liquid, or gas), but they don't always stay in the same state. For example, when you freeze water into ice cubes and then leave the ice out to melt, the water changes from liquid to solid and back into liquid. Afterward, the water is the same as before.

Physical Change

Changing state affects how the tiny particles inside materials behave. The particles can be atoms or molecules (a group of two or more atoms). In a solid, they are held together by strong forces (bonds). These loosen when the solid melts—that's why melting ice loses its shape. The particles in a liquid are held by looser bonds. These loosen more when the liquid evaporates (changes into a gas).

The dry ice used in special effects is frozen carbon dioxide. It turns back into gas so quickly that it misses out the liquid state. When a solid turns directly into a gas, it is called sublimation.

Temperature

The state of a material is controlled by temperature (how hot or cold it is). Materials need heat to change to a state where their particles move around more. Gas particles move more than liquid particles, and liquid particles move more than solid particles. So, solids melt and liquids evaporate when they are heated. The heat gives the particles more energy and weakens the bonds between them. Going the other way, gases condense and liquids freeze when they are cooled.

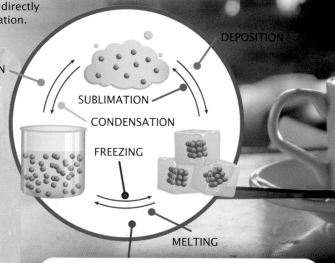

DEPOSITION

EVAPORATION

SUBLIMATION

CONDENSATION

FREEZING

MELTING

Freezing point and melting point are the same—the temperature where liquid turns into solid, or solid into liquid. Boiling point is the temperature where a liquid evaporates into gas, or the gas condenses into liquid.

DID YOU KNOW? Only one metal—mercury—is liquid at room temperature. It melts at a chilly -38.8°C (-37.9°F), compared with gold's 1,063°C (1,945°F).

The steam from a boiling kettle is water vapor escaping into the air.

Packed snow takes longer to absorb heat from the air, so a snowman melts more slowly than surrounding snow. Snow (water) has a melting point of 0°C (32°F).

Cooling water vapor condenses out of the air. It might run down the inside of the kettle or fog up the window.

The large bubbles of gas in the boiling kettle are water turning into water vapor (evaporating).

HALL OF FAME:
Aristotle
384–322 BCE

Aristotle was an ancient Greek philosopher (deep thinker) who believed that all matter was made up of four "elements"—earth, air, fire, and water. His ideas led to the belief that metals could change into gold (alchemy) and they influenced experimental chemistry for centuries.

Mixtures and Solutions

Do you like mashed potatoes or mashed turnips? Or a mixture? You might enjoy it, or you might want to take one ingredient out! In chemistry, pure substances are like the potatoes (or the turnips) on their own. Impure substances (mixtures) are like the two together.

Pure and Impure Substances

Chemically pure substances contain only one thing. It could be one element (the simplest chemicals) like gold, or one compound (a chemical made of other chemicals joined up) like table salt. You can't take anything out of a pure substance without changing it chemically. Impure substances are a mixture of elements or compounds. Importantly, the elements or compounds in the mixture are not chemically joined up, so they can be separated.

Air is a mixture of gases, including oxygen, nitrogen, and carbon dioxide.

This cool, carbonated drink is a mixture of liquid juice, solid ice cubes, and carbon dioxide gas. The carbon dioxide escapes as the fizzy bubbles rise to the top.

Mixing

If you shake peas into a bowl of water, you can still see the peas. But you can't always see the things in a mixture. When you stir sugar into tea, the sugar dissolves—the bonds between the sugar molecules (particles) break. The sugar seems to disappear, but it doesn't—you can taste the sweetness. When something dissolves in something else it makes a mixture called a solution. We can mix different combinations of solids, liquids, and gases.

DID YOU KNOW? "Pure" fruit juice has no added sugar, but it's not chemically pure, because it contains many compounds.

Salt is soluble because it dissolves in water. Salt is the solute (the solid that dissolves).

The water is the solvent (the liquid that something is dissolving in).

The salt–water mixture is a solution. Adding more salt makes the solution more concentrated. Adding more water makes it more diluted.

The metal pan is insoluble (it doesn't dissolve in water).

HALL OF FAME:
Mary Elliott Hill
1907–1969

Hill was a chemist and teacher who was one of the first African American women to be awarded a master's degree in chemistry. She encouraged students to study and teach chemistry despite their social difficulties. She and her husband worked together on making soluble compounds used in plastics production.

Diffusion and Brownian Motion

Materials are made of tiny particles that are atoms or molecules (two or more atoms bonded together). In fluids, the particles are weakly held and they move around. The movements make the particles diffuse (spread out evenly). Heat gives them energy to move faster and farther apart.

Brownian Motion

Particles in fluids move at random—they go in all directions by chance. This random movement is called Brownian motion, after the botanist Robert Brown, who first saw it in 1827. He looked through a microscope at pollen grains suspended in water and noticed that they moved randomly. Now we know they were being bumped around by the movements of water molecules that were too small for Brown to see.

When a dye is splashed into water, the particles are close together at first. There is a high concentration of color in one area and a low concentration everywhere else.

Water molecules are much smaller than pollen grains, but there are lots of them, so their high–energy bumping moves the pollen.

HALL OF FAME:
Albert Einstein
1879–1955

The great German–born physicist Einstein won the Nobel Prize for his work on electrically charged particles in 1921, but he had many more great ideas. He realized that the movements of pollen grains seen by Robert Brown must be due to collisions with unseen water particles—atoms.

Dissolving and Diffusion

A solid's particles are packed tightly. They vibrate on the spot, but they can't move past each other, so there's no diffusion inside a solid. But when a soluble (dissolvable) solid is mixed with a liquid, the bonds holding the solid's particles together are broken. This means that the solid breaks up into small pieces of the same substance. These molecules of the solid do diffuse—they spread out evenly through the liquid. This is called dissolving.

Gas particles have high energy and are fast-moving, so gases diffuse quickly to become evenly spread out.

The dye and water particles diffuse through each other until they are evenly mixed. Eventually, there will be an even concentration of color and water particles all through the solution.

The particles of both liquids move at random and bump into each other. This spreads the particles and mixes them up.

DID YOU KNOW? A glass thermometer works because heat makes the liquid inside expand and move up the scale.

15

Separating Solids from Mixtures

We mix materials all the time—think of putting together all the ingredients for a cake mix. Now think of unmixing them. Some mixtures are easier to separate than others! We can make different mixtures from solids, liquids, and gases, and the method we use to separate them depends on what's in the mixture.

Sieving and Filtering

Different-sized solids can be separated by sieving. The holes in the mesh of a sieve let small objects pass through and catch anything bigger. A filter is like a sieve and is used to separate pieces of solid from liquids. Straining boiled vegetables is filtering and so is straining coffee through filter paper—but the holes in the filter paper are much smaller than the holes in the vegetable strainer.

Gold is inert (unreactive), so the pure element is found naturally embedded in rocks. When the rock weathers (breaks up), the gold is washed away and gathers in the mud of rivers.

Evaporation

A solid dissolved in a liquid is a solution. We can separate a dissolved solid from its solvent by evaporation—the liquid is heated until it turns into a gas, and the pure solid is left behind. The amount of solid hasn't changed, because dissolving is a reversible change.

Traditional sea salt farmers let seawater evaporate in shallow pools. The salt crystals left behind are harvested by hand.

DID YOU KNOW? Records written in China over 4,700 years ago describe ways to extract and prepare sea salt to make food taste better.

Drew was a Black American surgeon who studied blood chemistry. He discovered that donated blood lasted longer if the red blood cells were separated from the plasma (liquid). His work on improved blood storage saved many lives in World War II, and he is known as the "Father of the Blood Bank."

River sediment (mud, sand, and gravel) can be passed through a sieve that lets water and smaller particles filter through, separating out the nuggets of gold.

Sieving and panning are both traditional methods of finding gold. In panning, the heavy gold sinks to the bottom of a solid pan, and other material is washed away over the edge.

Plastic rod

Black pepper particles

Black pepper and salt mixture

Ground pepper can be separated from salt by static electricity. A plastic rod is rubbed to give it a negative charge. The pepper is attracted to it, and it flies up and sticks to the rod.

Separating Solutions

A solution is a liquid mixture. Heating a solution until one liquid evaporates can take one component (part) out of the solution. The evaporated part can then be collected by turning it back into a liquid. This is called distillation.

Simple Distillation

Separating a liquid out of a solution is simple distillation. It purifies the liquid by removing the impurity (the other substance). To collect pure water from a salt and water solution, the solution is heated until it boils. The water component evaporates, leaving behind the salt crystals in the flask. The water vapor is cooled and collected—it is now safe to drink.

Distillation can be used to separate a liquid that boils at a low temperature from a mixture of liquids.

1

HALL OF FAME:
Alice Augusta Ball
1892–1916

Ball studied seed oils from the chaulmoogra tree to treat the infectious Hansen's disease (leprosy). She separated the oils by fractionation and made the active ingredients more soluble (dissolvable). The new, improved medicine could be injected, and it meant that patients were able to leave the leper colonies where they had been quarantined (isolated).

DID YOU KNOW? Oil refineries heat crude oil in fractionating towers. The world's tallest, in Nigeria, is 112 m (369 ft) high—as tall as a tower of 28 large elephants!

Fractional Distillation

Some solutions contain several different liquid components, or "fractions." The different fractions can be separated out and collected by fractional distillation. This process works because different liquids boil at different temperatures. They evaporate at different times during heating, so their vapors can be collected separately. Fractional distillation is used in oil refineries to separate crude oil into a range of fuels and compounds (chemicals) that are used in many industries.

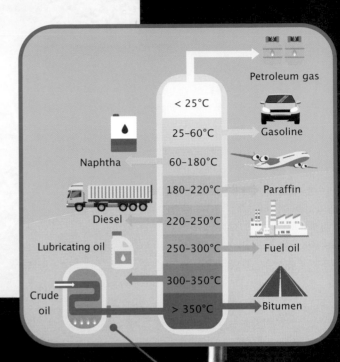

Petroleum gas

< 25°C

25–60°C — Gasoline

Naphtha — 60–180°C

180–220°C — Paraffin

Diesel — 220–250°C

Lubricating oil — 250–300°C — Fuel oil

300–350°C

Crude oil — > 350°C — Bitumen

Fractional distillation of crude oil gives us products such as bitumen for road surfaces and petrol (gasoline). Different fractions are used in various manufacturing industries.

2

3

4

1. The mixture is heated until the temperature reaches the boiling point of the first liquid. This liquid turns into a vapor.

2. The hot vapor flows through the condenser. This has a jacket of cold water flowing around it.

3. The vapor is cooled by the condenser and turns back into a liquid.

4. The pure liquid collects in the beaker.

Important Properties

Glass or transparent (see-through) plastic lets the light into a greenhouse.

Glass slippers and gingerbread houses are only good in fairy tales. In real life, we don't want brittle shoes or soggy houses! We choose materials with properties (qualities) that make them fit for the job. Hardness (how hard or soft something is), roughness, flexibility, and permeability (having pores that let liquid through) are some physical properties of materials.

Metals and Ceramics

Metals are good for building because they're hard and strong. They are also malleable (easily shaped), ductile (can be pulled into thin wires), and good conductors (carriers) of electricity and heat. Ceramics, such as porcelain and clay, are waterproof, strong, and not good conductors, but they are brittle—they break instead of bending. Ceramics are used for mugs, toilets, bricks, and car brakes.

These boats are made of fiberglass, a composite (combined) material made of plastic and glass fibers. Fiberglass is strong like glass and light like plastic.

A rubber band stretches because its molecules are long and tangled. When we pull it, the molecules straighten up and get longer. The stretching is reversible—the molecules bounce back.

Plastics and Rubber

Plastics are polymers (giant molecules) made from fossil fuels. Rubber is an elastic (stretchy) polymer. Plastics may be hard or soft, flexible or stiff, transparent or opaque. Plastic comes in many forms. It is so versatile (useful in lots of jobs) that we rely on it all the time.

20

King was the grandchild of slaves, and her father encouraged her education. She earned a master's degree in mathematics and chemistry at Cornell University and had a long career in science education. She taught chemistry to students at school and university, and even to soldiers during World War II. Many of her students had outstanding careers in science.

An apron may be made of waterproof cloth to keep the employee's clothes dry. A material that doesn't allow water to soak through it is "impermeable."

The plastic hose can bend around corners because it's flexible. The spray pieces are rigid (stiff) plastic or metal.

Plant pots are often made of a stiff, opaque (not see-through), recycled plastic. The large troughs may be made of wood, which is strong and permeable.

Ceramic tiles on the floor are smooth to walk on, hard-wearing, and easy to clean.

DID YOU KNOW? A diamond can scratch anything because diamond is the hardest natural substance on Earth. Diamond-edged tools are even used to drill rocks.

Conductors and Insulators

The properties of conductivity and insulation are to do with how easily a material lets energy pass through it. It can be thermal energy (heat) or electrical energy (electricity). Good conductors let energy pass through easily. Good insulators block the flow of energy.

Thermal Conduction

Heat conduction works because the tiny atoms and molecules that make up solids vibrate. When the material is heated, they vibrate faster. They bump against the atoms next to them, and so transfer the heat energy to cooler areas. Most metals are good heat conductors. Plastics, ceramics, and other non-metals like wood are good insulators.

Thermos bottles keep liquids hot or cold. This flask is metal, but it insulates because there's a vacuum (no air) between the bottle walls. This means that heat can't escape from hot liquids or get into cold liquids.

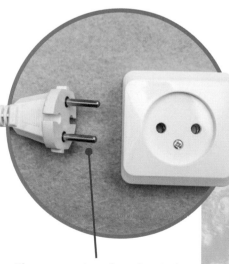

The copper pins of an electrical plug connect the wiring in the cable and the wall. The plug and wall socket are made of plastic to protect us from electric shocks.

Electrical Conduction

Electrical conduction works by a flow of electrons (the negatively charged part of atoms) through the material. Metals are good electrical conductors—electricity flows to appliances in our homes through metal wires. The wires are often copper, because this metal is a good conductor and also flexible and ductile (can be drawn out). Plastics are usually poor conductors of electrical energy.

DID YOU KNOW? Polar bear coats have hollow hairs for insulation. Scientists have copied the shape to make carbon tubes with heat-holding properties.

Heat passes through fluids (gases and liquids) by convection. Molecules in the heated air around the oven move around more, and they carry the heat to cooler areas.

Baking sheets are made of metal, because metals transfer heat easily from the oven to the food being cooked.

Padded oven gloves are good insulators. They protect our hands from the direct heat of the tray and from the hot air around the oven.

HALL OF FAME:
Alessandro Volta
1745–1827

Italian physicist Volta noticed that he felt a tingle when he touched two different metals to his tongue. He was detecting a current—the flow of electricity between the pieces of metal. He invented the battery by making a column of alternating (in turn) disks of zinc and silver separated by wet paper or cloth. His battery was the first source of electric current that did not need to be recharged.

Viscosity Oddities

A fun non-Newtonian fluid is Oobleck, made by mixing cornstarch (cornflour) and water.

How easily liquids flow is called viscosity. Water runs off surfaces easily—it has low viscosity. But a dollop of honey flows slowly off a spoon—the thick liquid is viscous. Viscous liquids flow slowly because there is friction (resistance) when the molecules (particles) inside them move over each other.

Viscosity in Newtonian Fluids

Isaac Newton found that (at unchanged temperatures) the viscosity of "normal" fluids stays the same even when they are pushed or pulled by outside forces. This means that shaking or stirring doesn't change how easily they flow. Fluids like this are "Newtonian fluids." Water is a Newtonian fluid—it flows as we expect, whether we sip it from a cup or throw ourselves into it in a swimming pool.

Oobleck gets its name from the sticky green substance in a storybook by Dr. Seuss.

Non-Newtonian Fluids

Colloids are mixtures with small particles of one substance spread through another substance. They can behave in surprising ways. Someone caught in quicksand (a colloid of sand in water) will float if they relax, but sink if they put force on the quicksand by struggling. Fluids like this, which behave differently when they're disturbed by forces, are "non-Newtonian fluids." Some, like quicksand, get runnier with forces, and some, like custard, get more viscous. It's said that if you jump into a swimming pool full of custard, you'll land on your feet instead of sinking!

Wiggle your leg out gently if it gets caught in quicksand.

DID YOU KNOW? When a frog grabs an insect on its tongue, its saliva gets runnier. It flows over the insect and then grips it by becoming viscous again.

Oobleck is a colloid of tiny particles of solid dispersed in water. It flows like a liquid, but you can squeeze it into a ball. It gets thicker when forces act on it.

If you prod Oobleck, the particles dispersed in the mixture don't have time to get out of the way of your finger. The force makes it act like a solid.

Ketchup comes out of the bottle more easily if you shake it first. The shaking forces make the thick substance act more like a liquid. It gets thinner when forces act on it.

25

Atomic Structure

Matter is made up of building blocks called atoms. Thinking of atoms as tiny balls helps explain how solids, liquids, and gases behave—but atoms also contain smaller, "subatomic" particles—protons, neutrons, and electrons. Different elements (the simplest chemicals) have different numbers of subatomic particles.

The Atomic Nucleus

The nucleus is in the middle of an atom. Protons and neutrons, which are almost 2,000 times heavier than electrons, are packed together inside the nucleus, so it is "massive" even though it's too small to see. Neutrons have no charge, and protons have a positive charge, making the nucleus positively charged. An element's atoms all have the same number of protons—this is its "atomic number."

Beryllium has atomic number 4. Its nucleus has four protons (light blue) and five neutrons (dark blue). Four electrons (green) are arranged in two surrounding energy shells.

Energy shells are stacked inside each other like Russian dolls. But the shells are not solid—only electromagnetic attraction holds the electrons close to the nucleus.

Electrons

Outside of the nucleus, the atom is mostly empty space. Electrons—very tiny particles with almost no mass and a negative charge—whiz around in energy "shells" (layers) surrounding the nucleus. Each shell can hold a set number of electrons, so atoms with more electrons have more shells. The equal and opposite charges of the protons and electrons attract each other—this electromagnetic force holds the electrons inside the atom. Atoms have the same number of electrons as protons, so the whole atom has no charge.

DID YOU KNOW? Protons and neutrons contain even tinier particles called quarks and gluons. Scientists know of 36 subatomic particles so far!

The total number of protons and neutrons in the nucleus is the atom's "mass number."

 Carbon 12
6 Protons
6 Neutrons
6 Electrons

 Carbon 13
6 Protons
7 Neutrons
6 Electrons

 Carbon 14
6 Protons
8 Neutrons
6 Electrons

Isotopes are forms of an element with different numbers of neutrons. A "normal" carbon atom nucleus—"Carbon 12"— has six neutrons, but other isotopes have seven or eight.

The first energy shell is closest to the nucleus. It can contain up to two electrons.

As the shells fill up with electrons, more shells are added. The heaviest atoms have over 100 electrons, in seven shells.

Bigger atoms have more shells, farther out from the nucleus. The second and third shells can contain up to eight electrons each.

Elements

Each element is made up of just one kind of atom. The atoms of different elements have different numbers of subatomic particles—protons, neutrons, and electrons—inside their atoms. These differences give the elements their individual properties (how they look and behave).

Names and Numbers

We know of 118 elements. Around 90 are found naturally, while the rest are made by scientists and are usually unstable and quickly decay (break up). Every element has a name and a symbol of one or two letters. For example, hydrogen has the symbol H, and lead has the symbol Pb. Each element is also identified by its atomic number—the number of protons inside one atom.

Air is a mixture of gases, including the elements nitrogen, oxygen, and argon. The element in an airship—helium—is a gas that is lighter than air.

Silicon oxide—a compound of oxygen and silicon—makes up most of Earth's crust as rocks or sand. Aluminum, iron, and calcium are the next three most common elements in the crust.

All Our Resources

At room temperature, only two elements are liquids—mercury and bromine—while 11 are gases. The rest are solids, and most of them are metals. Some elements—like nuggets of gold—occur naturally in pure form, but most are found in impure form, as compounds with other elements. Elements and their compounds make up the minerals and rocks of the Earth's crust.

HALL OF FAME:
Ida Noddack
née Tacke
1896–1978

The element rhenium was first isolated in 1925 in Germany, by Ida Tacke, Otto Berg, and Walter Noddack, Ida's future husband. Rhenium has a very high melting point and is now used in aircraft engines. Ida was also the first to suggest that atoms bombarded by neutrons might split into smaller atoms. Four years later, nuclear fission was shown to be possible.

Copper is a "trace" element—a tiny amount in your body keeps you healthy.

Gold is very unreactive—it does not react with air and tarnish (go dull). It is used in medicine and in tooth fillings, and also in some electronic devices.

Silver is an excellent conductor (carrier) of heat and electricity. It reflects light well and is used in mirrors and solar panels.

DID YOU KNOW? The most recently discovered element, tennessine, was made in a laboratory in 2010. Very few atoms were made, and they decayed quickly.

Molecules

Atoms like to stick together! Only a few—the noble gases—hang around on their own. Most of them bond together with other atoms to make molecules. Molecules can be two atoms, or larger groups, and sometimes they are giant molecular structures. A crystal is a structure where the atoms or molecules join up in a regular, repeating pattern, often shown off in gems like diamonds.

A pencil drawing is made of graphite. Both graphite and diamond are giant molecular structures of carbon.

Diatomic Molecules

There are two atoms in diatomic molecules. If the atoms are identical, the molecule is "homonuclear." Elements with atoms that pair up in this way are "diatomic elements." The bond is made by sharing electrons, which fill up the atoms' energy shells with the most electrons they can hold. A hydrogen atom has one electron, but its shell can hold two—so two hydrogen atoms share their two electrons.

Hydrogen is a diatomic element. By pairing up and sharing their electrons to make a bond, two hydrogen atoms make a stable, homonuclear molecule.

HALL OF FAME: Rosalind Franklin 1920–1958

British scientist Franklin studied molecules, using X-ray crystallography. She helped to show he double helix (spiral) structure of the biological molecule, DNA (deoxyribonucleic acid). She also made important discoveries about the structure of viruses, as well as about the different forms of carbon in coal and graphite. Her work on carbon paved the way for the development of useful carbon fiber technologies.

DID YOU KNOW? The largest uncut diamond found, the Cullinan, measured 10.1 x 6.35 x 5.9 cm (4 x 2.5 x 2.3 inches). It was cut into over 100 gemstones.

Allotropes

The crystals of some elements are simple—they only contain one kind of atom—yet surprising. Their atoms join together in different ways to make different allotropes. Two allotropes of carbon are diamond and graphite (pencil "lead.") Diamond and graphite seem like different elements, because the way their atoms are arranged makes them look and behave very differently.

Diamond is the hardest natural substance on Earth. The best crystals can be cut into costly gemstones, but diamond is also used in industrial tools.

Diamond	Graphite	Fullerene
Tetrahedral	Trigonal planer	Spherical

The molecular sheets in graphite are weakly bonded, so graphite is softer than diamond, where bonds are strong in all directions. Another allotrope—buckminsterfullerene—has atoms in a sphere.

Graphite looks gray and dull. It is soft and used in pencils—its molecules slide over each other and easily rub off to leave a mark on paper.

Crystals of the element sulfur can be shaped like four-sided pyramids, or as long needles. The different forms are allotropes.

Compounds

Compounds are molecules with more than one kind of atom. They are made when the atoms of different elements react and bond together. The different chemicals in a compound can only be separated by a chemical change.

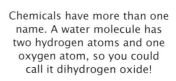

Compound Properties

No atoms are lost when chemicals react. This means the chemicals at the start (the reactants) and at the end (the products) contain the same atoms in different combinations. The products have new properties—they look and behave differently to the reactants. When you drink water, you are drinking a compound of hydrogen and oxygen, which are both gases in the air. And when you lick salt, you are eating a compound of chlorine (a gas) and sodium (a metal).

Chemicals have more than one name. A water molecule has two hydrogen atoms and one oxygen atom, so you could call it dihydrogen oxide!

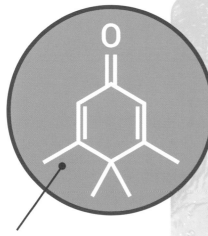

The structural chemical formula of 3,4,4,5-tetramethyl-2,5-cyclohexadien-1-one looks a bit like a penguin. Its common name is penguinone.

Names and Formulae

Some compounds contain many elements and have complicated names to describe them. Luckily scientists give chemicals simpler common names too. They also have a clever, short way of describing compounds—chemical formulae. Every element has a symbol of one or two letters, and these make up the chemical formulae of all possible compounds. The formula for water is H_2O, and this shows that the molecule has one oxygen and two hydrogen atoms. Another kind of formula, drawn to show the links between atoms, is the structural chemical formula.

DID YOU KNOW? Made in 2014, the largest molecule, PG5, contains 17 million atoms of carbon, nitrogen, and oxygen. At 10 nanometers, it's as big as a virus.

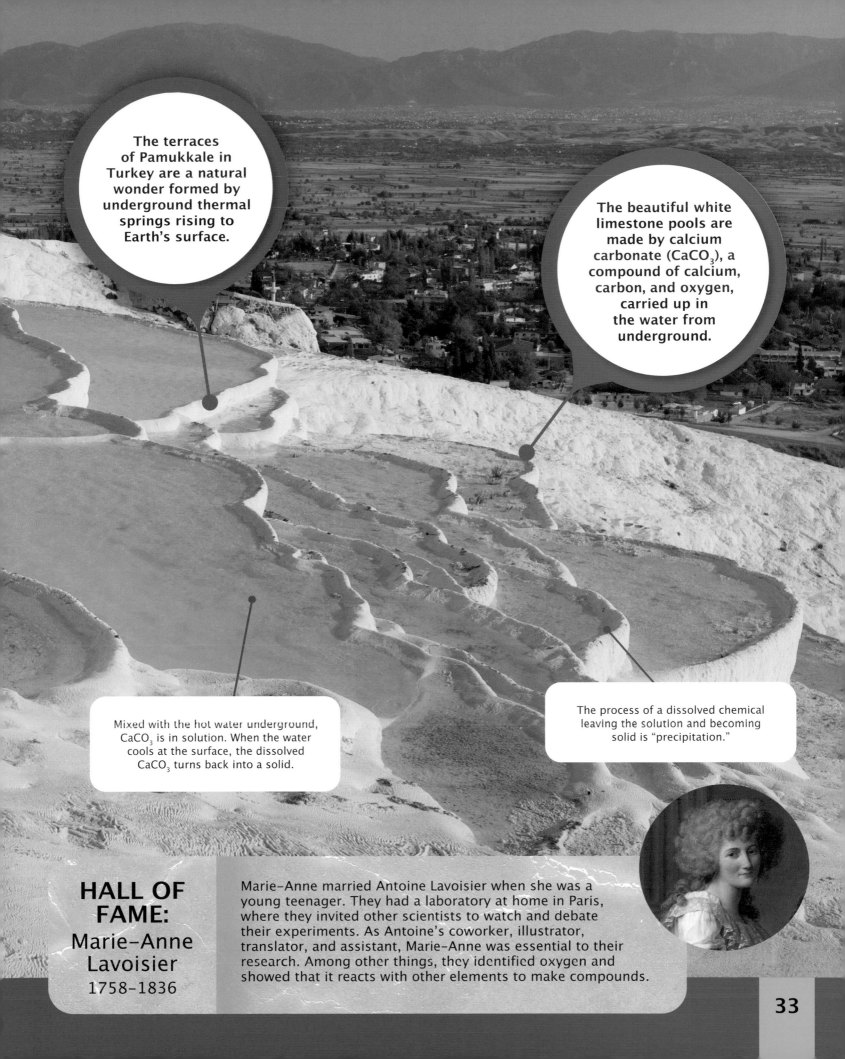

The terraces of Pamukkale in Turkey are a natural wonder formed by underground thermal springs rising to Earth's surface.

The beautiful white limestone pools are made by calcium carbonate ($CaCO_3$), a compound of calcium, carbon, and oxygen, carried up in the water from underground.

Mixed with the hot water underground, $CaCO_3$ is in solution. When the water cools at the surface, the dissolved $CaCO_3$ turns back into a solid.

The process of a dissolved chemical leaving the solution and becoming solid is "precipitation."

HALL OF FAME:
Marie-Anne
Lavoisier
1758–1836

Marie-Anne married Antoine Lavoisier when she was a young teenager. They had a laboratory at home in Paris, where they invited other scientists to watch and debate their experiments. As Antoine's coworker, illustrator, translator, and assistant, Marie-Anne was essential to their research. Among other things, they identified oxygen and showed that it reacts with other elements to make compounds.

Covalent Bonds

An atom is a nucleus orbited by electrons in energy shells. Each shell can hold a certain number of electrons and must be full before another shell can be added. When atoms react and join up to make a molecule, a bond is made by the electrons in their outermost shells. How many bonds an atom can make is its "valency."

The Shared Bond

Atoms are most stable (unreactive) when their shells are full, so you can think of atoms as "wanting" to fill up with electrons. They can do it by "sharing" their electrons, and this makes a covalent bond. The first shell of an atom holds up to two electrons. This explains why the two smallest atoms, with only one shell—hydrogen and helium—behave differently. A hydrogen atom, with one electron, readily shares it with another atom. But a helium atom has two electrons, so it doesn't react because it is already stable.

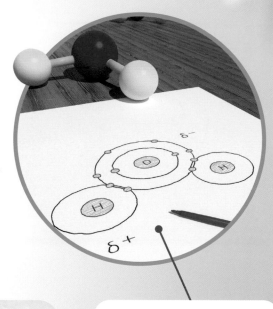

In a water molecule, the electrons donated by the oxygen atom fill up the hydrogens' single shells. The electrons donated by the hydrogen atoms fill up the oxygen's second shell.

Double Bonds

A pair of electrons shared between two atoms makes a single covalent bond. Some atoms can also make a double bond, by sharing two pairs of electrons. They can do this because the second and third shells can each hold up to eight electrons. An oxygen atom has six electrons in its second shell, so it "wants" two more (it has a valency of two). Two oxygen atoms can each donate (give) two electrons to share between them, making eight electrons for each of their outer shells.

Four electrons shared by two oxygen atoms create a double bond in an oxygen molecule. The nuclei, with eight protons and eight neutrons each, remain unchanged.

34

Pauling, born in Oregon, USA, was one of the first scientists to use quantum physics—where subatomic particles can behave like waves—to describe how atoms make bonds in molecules. He was awarded the Nobel Prize in Chemistry for this work in 1954. He went on to be awarded the Nobel Peace Prize in 1962 for his efforts to ban nuclear weapons tests and end the threat of nuclear war.

The hydrogen and carbon atoms in the candle wax make new covalent bonds with oxygen, producing carbon dioxide gas and water vapor.

Candles are made of paraffin (petroleum) wax, which is the fuel when the candle is lit.

The candle burns, producing heat and light, until all the wax is used up. The reaction is combustion—the burning of a fuel in oxygen.

Wax is a hydrocarbon—it has hydrogen and carbon atoms. When the candle burns, the heat melts the wax, which then turns into a vapor. Its molecular bonds are broken.

DID YOU KNOW? In quantum physics, it seems an electron can spin in two directions at once and can affect another electron even across the galaxy. Weird!

35

Ionic Bonds

Atoms stick together when an electrical force made by the electrons in their outermost energy shells makes a bond between them. In covalent bonds, the electrons are shared, but in ionic bonds the electrons move from atom to atom.

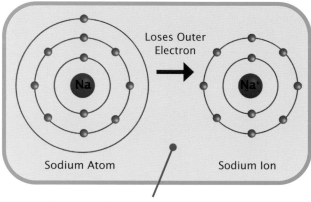

Sodium Atom   Sodium Ion

Loses Outer Electron

A sodium atom has only one electron in its outer (third) shell. It readily gives it up, because then its second shell becomes its outer shell, and it has the full, stable number of eight electrons.

Ions

An atom usually has no charge—the negative charge of its electrons balances out the positive charge of its nucleus. When an atom loses or gains an electron, it loses or gains some negative charge and becomes a charged particle called an "ion." If an electron moves away from an atom, it leaves an ion with a positive charge—a "cation." An atom that gets an extra electron becomes a negative ion—an "anion."

Ionic Lattices

The opposite charges of cations and anions attract each other by electrostatic force, and this makes an ionic bond. Compounds containing ionic bonds are crystals with a regular, repeating pattern of negative and positive ions in an ionic lattice structure. The electrostatic forces act in all directions, making ionic lattices strong. The compounds have no overall charge, because the negative and positive charges balance each other out. They usually have high melting and boiling points, because a lot of energy is needed to break all the ionic bonds.

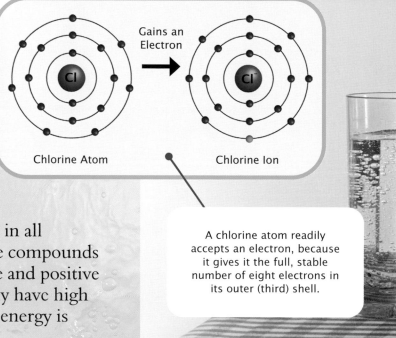

Chlorine Atom   Chlorine Ion

Gains an Electron

A chlorine atom readily accepts an electron, because it gives it the full, stable number of eight electrons in its outer (third) shell.

DID YOU KNOW? Our nerve cells use sodium and other ions to send electrochemical messages that travel at up to 288 km/h (180 mph)!

A salt crystal is a cubic structure of alternating sodium ions and chlorine ions. The sodium ions are positive (Na^+), and the chlorine ions are negative (Cl^-).

Both sodium (a metal) and chlorine (a gas) can be dangerous chemicals, but they combine to make an essential, tasty part of our diet.

Electrons are tightly held in ionic bonds in metal compounds. This is why sodium chloride doesn't conduct electricity—which is the flow of electrons—but the pure metal, sodium, does.

The salt we use to season our food is sodium chloride. It is a giant ionic structure of sodium and chlorine ions.

HALL OF FAME:
Michael Faraday
1791–1867

The great English scientist Faraday found that some nonconducting compounds, like sodium chloride, would conduct electricity when dissolved in water. He thought that electricity broke compounds into charged particles, and he used the terms ion (meaning "wanderer"), cation, and anion to describe them. His work was the basis of later scientists' discovery of electrons and their roles in both chemical bonds and electricity.

Reactions

When substances react together, the chemicals before the reaction (the reactants) make new chemicals (products) with new properties. Their atoms rearrange—they break their bonds and make new ones. No atoms are lost, so the same atoms are combined differently in the reactants and the products.

Atoms bond together like a group of dancers. They can hold hands (bond), and they can let go, move around, and find new partners.

Chemical Equations

A word equation describes a reaction. For example, the word equation for the reaction of carbon and oxygen to make carbon dioxide is:

carbon + oxygen ⟶ carbon dioxide

The chemical equation tells us more. It uses chemical symbols and formulae to show the type and number of atoms in the molecules of the reactants and products:

$C + O_2 \longrightarrow CO_2$

It shows that one atom of carbon reacts with two atoms of oxygen to make a carbon dioxide molecule containing one carbon and two oxygen atoms. The equation is "balanced," with three atoms before the arrow and three atoms after it.

This equation shows that two atoms of sodium and two molecules of water produce two molecules of sodium hydroxide and a molecule (two atoms) of hydrogen.

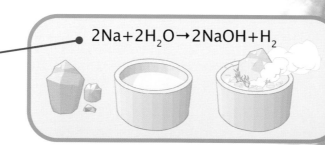

$2Na + 2H_2O \rightarrow 2NaOH + H_2$

HALL OF FAME:
Antoine Lavoisier
1743–1794

Lavoisier developed a theory of chemical reactivity based on experiments. He showed that as much matter exists after a reaction as before, and in 1789, he published a book stating the Law of the Conservation of Mass for the first time. The book also introduced a new way of naming compounds that is still the basis of chemical names today. Lavoisier was executed during the French Revolution.

When copper wire is suspended in a clear silver nitrate solution, copper atoms take the place of silver and change the solution to blue copper nitrate. Displaced silver forms crystals on the wire.

Reactivity

Reactivity is how readily a chemical reacts with others. Some metals, like sodium, are so reactive that they are only found as compounds in nature. Others, like gold, are not at all reactive. In the reactivity series of metals (a list of metals from most reactive to least reactive), sodium is more reactive than copper, which is more reactive than silver, which is more reactive than gold. A more reactive metal will replace a less reactive metal in a compound in solution. This is displacement.

The members of the group stay the same, even when they change partners.

Some members change partners more easily than others.

DID YOU KNOW? Chemical reactions keep us alive—that's biochemistry. Trillions of biochemical reactions are happening in your body right now.

Reversible and Irreversible Changes

In a chemical reaction, the reactants' atoms rearrange to make the products. Some reactions are reversible; for example, nitrogen dioxide gas breaks down into nitrogen monoxide and oxygen when heated, and changes back when cooled. Other reactions, like burning and corrosion, are irreversible—it's impossible to get the original reactants back.

Cooking and Combustion

A cook can't unbake a cake, because the ingredients have been permanently, chemically changed. Baking a cake involves reactions such as thermal decomposition, which is breaking apart (rather than burning or melting) a substance by heat. Combustion—when a fuel is burned in air—is another useful, irreversible reaction. The fuel, such as wood, reacts with oxygen in the air to release energy in the form of light and heat—but we can't turn the ash back into wood afterward.

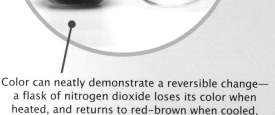

Color can neatly demonstrate a reversible change—a flask of nitrogen dioxide loses its color when heated, and returns to red–brown when cooled.

HALL OF FAME:
William Jacob Knox
1904–1995

Knox earned his Chemistry PhD at Massachusetts Institute of Technology (MIT). During World War II, he was a supervisor in the Manhattan Project, using the corrosive gas, uranium hexafluoride, to separate isotopes. Later, he became only the second Black chemist to work at the Eastman Kodak company. The lifelong racial prejudice he faced inspired him to fight for civil rights, and he set up scholarships to help minority students.

DID YOU KNOW? The planet Mars is rusty—it looks red because iron in its soil reacted with oxygen billions of years ago, when the planet had liquid water.

Corrosion and rusting

Corrosion is an oxidation reaction in which a metal oxidizes—gains oxygen from the air. It is an example of permanent change and can be a problem in buildings, because the metal gets weaker as it continues to change into the metal oxide. Rusting is the type of corrosion that happens when iron is exposed to oxygen in air or water.

Iron reacts with oxygen to produce iron oxide—rust.

The statue is made of iron, covered with copper sheets. Copper reacts with oxygen in the air to form copper oxide.

The copper oxide has reacted with carbon dioxide, sulfur, and salt in the air to create the copper compounds that make the blue-green pigment, verdigris.

The Statue of Liberty, with its pedestal, is 93 m (305 ft) high. It has stood on Liberty Island, USA, since 1886. The blue-green statue was once bright red-brown, like a new copper penny.

The verdigris keeps the copper underneath from reacting more—so the statue is protected by the corrosion on the surface.

Exothermic and Endothermic Reactions

When chemicals react, their atoms are rearranged—their bonds are broken and new ones made. Energy is taken in when bonds are broken, and released when they are formed. The difference in the energy absorbed and released by all the bonds makes the total reaction endothermic or exothermic. The energy is usually (but not always) heat.

Nitric acid is a compound of hydrogen, nitrogen, and oxygen. It is a strong oxidizing chemical (it provides oxygen for reactions), and it can produce explosions—violent exothermic reactions.

Exothermic Reactions

Exothermic reactions release energy overall, so they can feel warm. Many oxidation reactions—where a substance gains oxygen—are exothermic. Disposable hand warmers use a surprising exothermic oxidation reaction—rusting! The pouch contains separated water and iron powder. When it's activated, the iron reacts with oxygen in the water, producing iron oxide (rust) and heat. Respiration is another exothermic reaction. It produces energy for your body to use.

When you snap a glow stick, you start an exothermic reaction that releases energy in the form of light.

DID YOU KNOW? Composting is exothermic. Australian brush turkeys don't sit on their eggs; they build a compost pile of decaying vegetation that heats up.

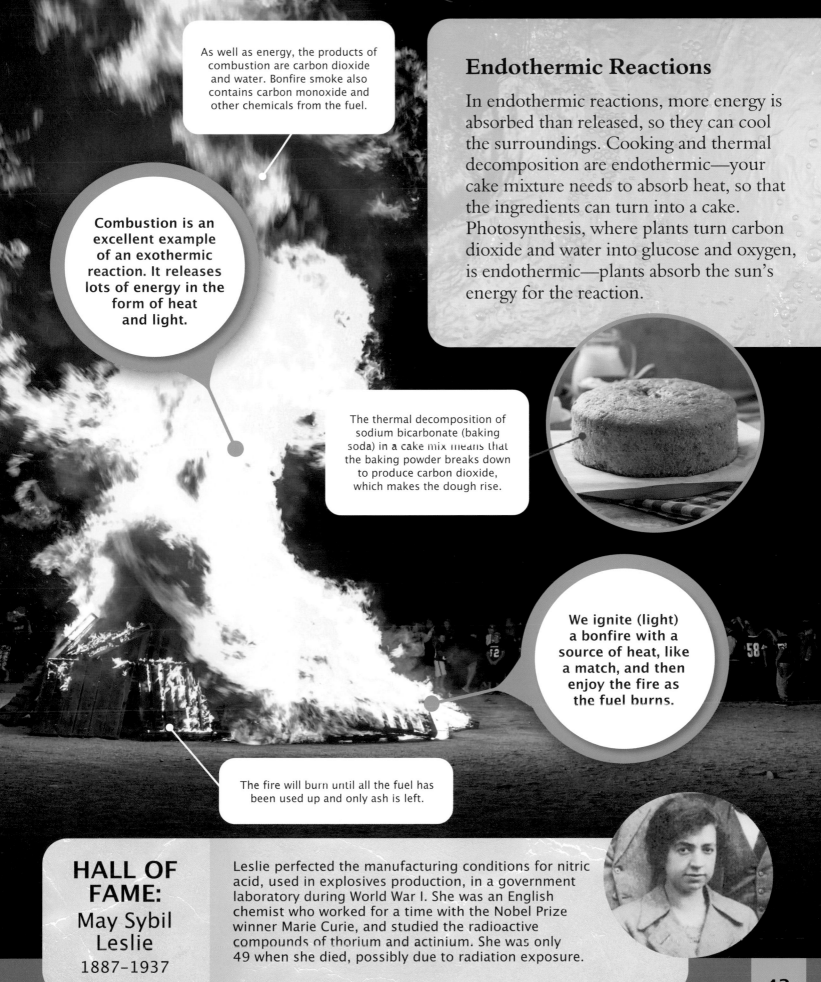

As well as energy, the products of combustion are carbon dioxide and water. Bonfire smoke also contains carbon monoxide and other chemicals from the fuel.

Combustion is an excellent example of an exothermic reaction. It releases lots of energy in the form of heat and light.

Endothermic Reactions

In endothermic reactions, more energy is absorbed than released, so they can cool the surroundings. Cooking and thermal decomposition are endothermic—your cake mixture needs to absorb heat, so that the ingredients can turn into a cake. Photosynthesis, where plants turn carbon dioxide and water into glucose and oxygen, is endothermic—plants absorb the sun's energy for the reaction.

The thermal decomposition of sodium bicarbonate (baking soda) in a cake mix means that the baking powder breaks down to produce carbon dioxide, which makes the dough rise.

We ignite (light) a bonfire with a source of heat, like a match, and then enjoy the fire as the fuel burns.

The fire will burn until all the fuel has been used up and only ash is left.

HALL OF FAME:
May Sybil Leslie
1887–1937

Leslie perfected the manufacturing conditions for nitric acid, used in explosives production, in a government laboratory during World War I. She was an English chemist who worked for a time with the Nobel Prize winner Marie Curie, and studied the radioactive compounds of thorium and actinium. She was only 49 when she died, possibly due to radiation exposure.

Speeding Up Reactions

Atoms and molecules react when they collide—but only if they carry enough energy to break their bonds. Increasing either the number of collisions or the energy of the particles speeds up a chemical reaction. You can do this by raising the temperature or pressure, or by adding more reactant—so that there are more particles to collide.

Magical Catalysts

Catalysts speed up reactions. They don't change the products of the reaction, and they aren't changed themselves, so they can be used again and again. They make reactions happen faster, so more product can be made in less time. They also make reactions happen at lower temperatures, which is cheaper. Only a very small amount of catalyst is needed for a reaction. This all makes catalysts very useful in manufacturing industries.

Enzymes are biological catalysts that speed up biochemical reactions in living organisms. The enzymes in yeast—a fungus—help bread rise.

HALL OF FAME:
Edith Flanigen
1929–present

Flanigen is an American chemist and inventor of molecular sieves, natural and synthetic materials used as filters and catalysts in industry. Among the materials she developed is "zeolite Y," used to break down crude oil and make oil refining cleaner and safer. Flanigen received many awards and patents for her work in cleaner fuels and environmental cleanup. She was awarded the US National Medal of Technology and Innovation in 2014.

DID YOU KNOW? Scientists don't always know how catalysts work, but they are using computers to develop new ones that may revolutionize electric car batteries.

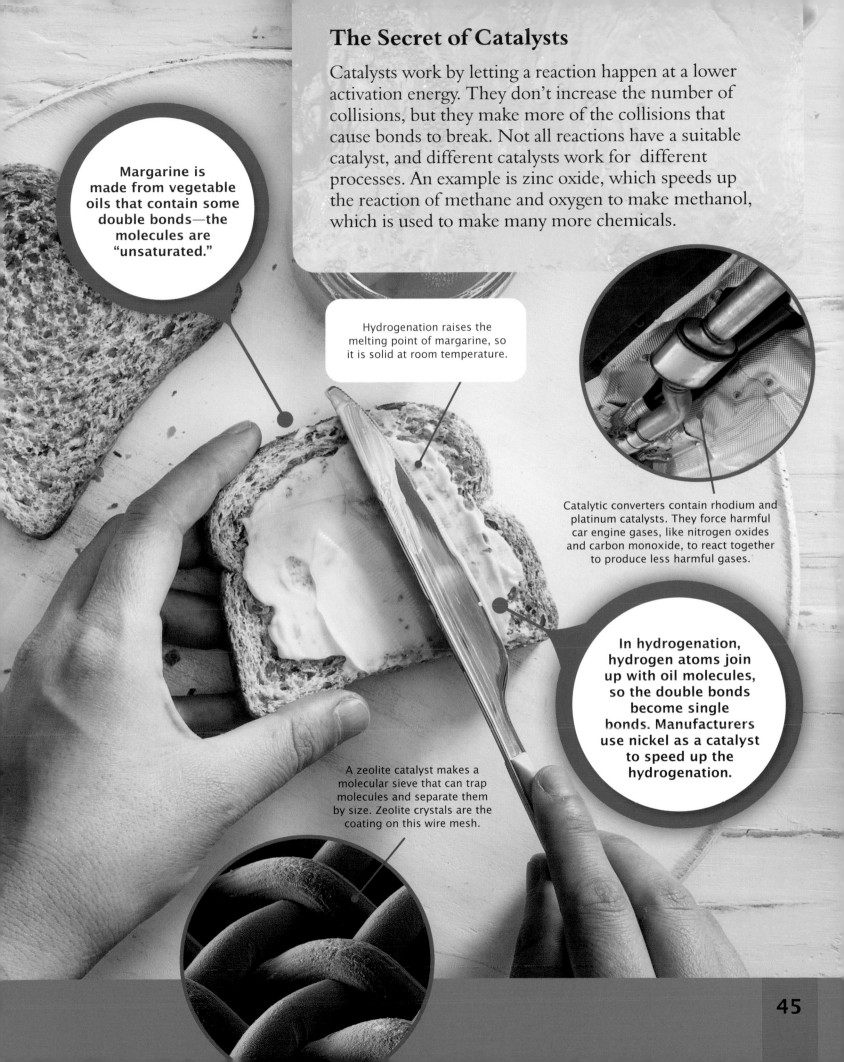

The Secret of Catalysts

Catalysts work by letting a reaction happen at a lower activation energy. They don't increase the number of collisions, but they make more of the collisions that cause bonds to break. Not all reactions have a suitable catalyst, and different catalysts work for different processes. An example is zinc oxide, which speeds up the reaction of methane and oxygen to make methanol, which is used to make many more chemicals.

Margarine is made from vegetable oils that contain some double bonds—the molecules are "unsaturated."

Hydrogenation raises the melting point of margarine, so it is solid at room temperature.

Catalytic converters contain rhodium and platinum catalysts. They force harmful car engine gases, like nitrogen oxides and carbon monoxide, to react together to produce less harmful gases.

In hydrogenation, hydrogen atoms join up with oil molecules, so the double bonds become single bonds. Manufacturers use nickel as a catalyst to speed up the hydrogenation.

A zeolite catalyst makes a molecular sieve that can trap molecules and separate them by size. Zeolite crystals are the coating on this wire mesh.

The Periodic Table

The Periodic Table neatly displays all the elements by the size of their building blocks—their atoms. The atoms in different elements contain different numbers of subatomic particles—protons, neutrons, and electrons. This means that we can sort the elements by the number of protons in the nucleus of one atom.

Order of Size

The elements are placed in Periods (rows) and Groups (columns). Hydrogen, in the first square in Period 1, has only one proton and one electron. Helium is a bit bigger, with two protons and two electrons. Then comes lithium, which starts Period 2. The atoms get heavier along the Periods and down the Groups, until the final square in Period 7, Group 8. This is organesson, the most giant of atoms, with 118 protons.

All the elements in one Period (row) have the same number of energy shells—orbits of electrons around the nucleus. Period 2 elements all have two shells.

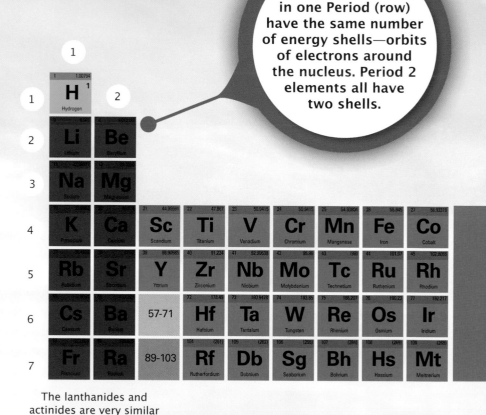

KEY

- ALKALI METALS
- ALKALINE EARTH METALS
- TRANSITION METALS
- BASIC METALS
- SEMI-METALS
- NON-METALS
- HALOGENS
- NOBLE GASES
- LANTHANIDES
- ACTINIDES

The lanthanides and actinides are very similar elements squeezed in between squares 57 and 71, and squares 89 and 103.

Elements such as the transition metals and non-metals are also grouped together by their similar properties.

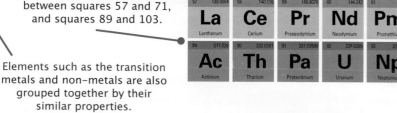

All the elements in a Group have the same number of electrons in their outer energy shells. This makes them look and behave in similar ways. Group 7 elements all have seven electrons in the outer shell.

What It Tells Us

One square gives the name and symbol of an element, with its "atomic number"—that is, number of protons (which is the same as its number of electrons). It also shows the relative weight of the atom—its "atomic mass"—which relates to the mass of its protons plus neutrons. Atomic mass has a decimal point because it's an average of different isotopes with different neutron counts. Other versions of the Periodic Table may give an atom's "mass number"—number of protons plus neutrons—which is always a whole number.

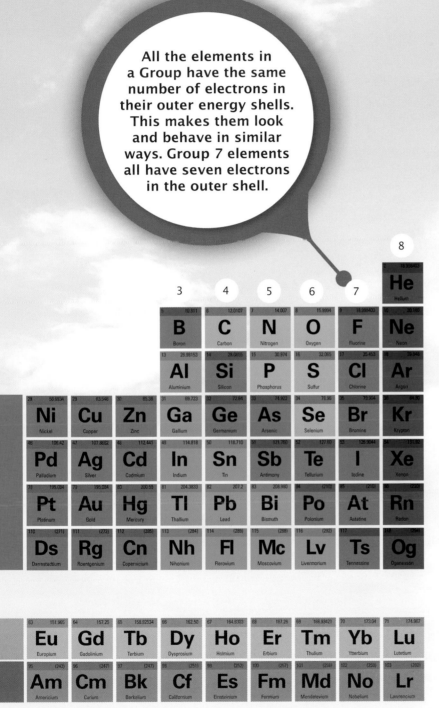

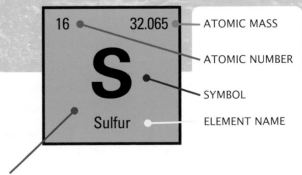

ATOMIC MASS
ATOMIC NUMBER
SYMBOL
ELEMENT NAME

Sulfur (S) has 16 protons in one atom. Its usual mass number is 32, showing that it has 16 neutrons (32 minus 16).

DID YOU KNOW? People in the Middle Ages swallowed antimony (element 51) to treat constipation. The antimony pill could be retrieved afterward and used again!

47

Element Groups

The Periodic Table ranks the elements' atoms in size order by number of protons, which is the same as their number of electrons. Atoms have energy shells that hold up to a certain number of electrons. The first (innermost) shell can hold two electrons. When it's full, a second shell outside of it holds up to eight electrons. Successive shells are farther out from the nucleus. Shells are most stable (unreactive) when they hold the most electrons they can.

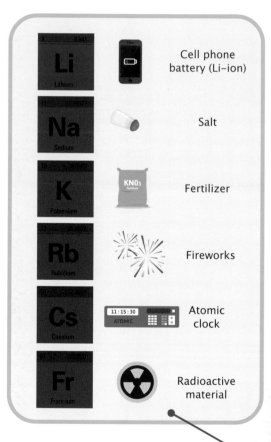

Cell phone battery (Li–ion)

Salt

Fertilizer

Fireworks

Atomic clock

Radioactive material

Group 1 elements—the alkali metals—have similar properties, but they are used in lots of different industries.

The Outer Shell Electrons

Elements in Periodic Table Groups (columns) behave alike, because of their pattern of electrons. For example, each Group 1 element (going down the Group) has one more energy shell than the one before—so lithium has two, sodium has three, and francium has seven shells—but they all have an outermost shell with just one solitary electron. This makes them behave alike, since they all react readily to give up the solitary electron. Elements in other Groups are also alike, because they have the same number of electrons in their outer shells.

All alkali metals react with water, giving off hydrogen gas and heat. The reaction gets more violent the farther down Group 1 the element sits.

HALL OF FAME:
Margeurite Catherine Perey
1909–1975

In 1939, francium became the last naturally occurring element to be discovered, and it was the only element to be discovered solely by a woman. Perey was separating radioactive elements when she found one that fit the gap at atomic number 87 in Mendeleev's Periodic Table. She named it *francium* after her home country, France.

Alkali Metals

The alkali metals are the Group 1 elements—lithium, sodium, potassium, rubidium, and caesium, plus radioactive francium. They are shiny metals, soft enough to cut with a knife. They all react readily with other chemicals, but the ones lower down the Group are more reactive than those above. They all react with cold water by releasing heat—an exothermic reaction. They react with some non-metals to form white, soluble, crystalline salts. For example, sodium reacts with chlorine to form sodium chloride—the salt in our food.

Alkali metals react with oxygen in the air to make metal oxides. The bright, newly cut surface of sodium tarnishes (goes dull) in moments. Potassium reacts even faster!

Violent reactivity makes the alkali metals very dangerous. Rubidium and caesium would explode in water.

Potassium has a spectacular reaction. The hydrogen gas it produces bursts into flame, and the potassium sparks, catches fire, and may make a small explosion.

Lithium and sodium react less violently than potassium. They whiz around on the surface, fizzing with hydrogen gas bubbles, until all the metal is used up.

DID YOU KNOW? Caesium atomic clocks are the most accurate clocks in the world, losing or gaining just one second in 1,400,000 years!

Tiny Hydrogen

The tiny atoms of hydrogen and helium were the first to form after the Big Bang. Hydrogen is the smallest atom, with one proton, one electron, and no neutrons. Hydrogen is often shown at the top of Group 1—but it's nothing like the solid, soft, shiny alkali metals of Group 1. Hydrogen is unique.

Highly Reactive

Pure hydrogen is rare on Earth. It is very reactive, so it's usually found in compounds with other elements. It is a nontoxic (not poisonous) gas, with no color, smell, or taste. It's the lightest element, used in weather balloons that gather information high in the atmosphere. It readily explodes with oxygen, and burns in air to produce water and energy. Hydrogen is so reactive because it easily shares or gives up its solitary electron.

LH2
LIQUID HYDROGEN

Hydrogen gas must be pressurized (compressed) or liquefied to store and move. It becomes liquid when it's supercooled to −253°C (−423°F). This is expensive and can be dangerous.

Every shuttle flight to the International Space Station uses about 2,250,000 liters (500,000 gallons) of hydrogen liquid as fuel.

Powerful Hydrogen

We wouldn't be here without hydrogen. Life-giving water is made from hydrogen and oxygen atoms. With carbon and other atoms, hydrogen forms the organic chemicals that make up every living thing. Hydrogen gives us fuel via the hydrocarbon molecules of crude oil and natural gas. Pure hydrogen is also becoming more important as a renewable, clean fuel in vehicles and aircraft. Hydrogen takes us into space—it has been used as rocket fuel since the beginning of space exploration in the 1950s.

DID YOU KNOW? Hydrogen is the most abundant element in the Universe—its atoms make up over 70 percent of the total mass of matter.

The earliest chemists were called alchemists. Paracelsus was an alchemist who established the use of chemicals such as mercury and sulfur in medicines. He observed that poisons could also heal, at a different dosage. Paracelsus is believed to have discovered hydrogen without realizing it, when he noticed that iron filings in sulfuric acid produced gas bubbles that could burn.

As hydrogen-fueled cars are being improved, some roadside fuel stations have hydrogen pumps next to the more common gas pumps that use fossil fuels.

We need clean energy alternatives like hydrogen cars, because fossil fuels contribute to climate change and they will run out.

Compressed hydrogen gas is squashed into the vehicle's fuel tank. When it's fed into the fuel cells, it reacts with oxygen, producing energy which is turned into electricity.

Electricity runs the car's engine. The only other product is water, so there are no polluting emissions.

Alkaline Earth Metals

The alkaline earth metals—beryllium, magnesium, calcium, strontium, barium, and radium—are the elements in Group 2 of the Periodic Table. Their atoms have two electrons in their outer energy shell. This makes them very reactive, although not as reactive as the alkali metals in Group 1.

Increasing Reactivity

Like the alkali metals, the alkaline earth metals are silvery or gray, and their reactivity increases as you go down the Group. Beryllium, at the top, is the least reactive. It needs a very high temperature before it can react with water. Magnesium, the next element down the Group, fizzes a little in cold water, while the reaction is more and more vigorous for calcium, then strontium, and then barium.

Beryllium and magnesium are used in metal alloys (mixtures) in aircraft and cars because they are light. Barium, which is much heavier, helps doctors see inside patients' bodies with X-rays.

Be — Beryllium — Spacecraft structure

Mg — Magnesium — Banana

Ca — Calcium — Shell

Sr — Strontium — Fireworks

Ba — Barium — X-ray

Ra — Radium — Radioactive material

Magnesium helps the enzymes in our bodies to work, so it's important to eat plenty of magnesium-rich foods.

Alkaline Medicines

The alkaline earth metals get their name because their compounds make solutions with water that are "alkaline" (above pH 7 on the scale of acidity/alkalinity; see pages 74–75). Milk of magnesia is a suspension of magnesium hydroxide (H_2MgO_2). It's used as an alkaline medicine to treat indigestion because it neutralizes (cancels out) the stomach acids that cause the pain.

DID YOU KNOW? The hands of bedside clocks used to be painted with glow-in-the-dark paints containing radioactive radium, all the way up until the 1960s.

Alkaline earth metals are so reactive that they can only exist naturally as compounds. The gemstone emerald is a compound of beryllium. Small amounts of chromium make it green.

Marine snails make seashells from calcium carbonate. Other invertebrates like corals and crabs also build protective skeletons from calcium compounds.

Calcium is essential for all living things. Vertebrates, like us, use calcium compounds to build strong bones and teeth. The main compound in bones is calcium phosphate.

Pollutants such as sulfur dioxide make "acid rain." This softens the skeletons and shells of sea creatures, and is harmful to life both in the oceans and on land.

HALL OF FAME:
Isabella Cortese
Sixteenth Century

Cortese was a well-traveled Italian alchemist who wrote the first book of cosmetic recipes, published in 1561. The book gave advice on running a household and how to make medicines and cosmetics, as well as discussing how metals might be turned into gold. It was very popular with the public and was republished several times.

The Halogens

That familiar swimming-pool smell is from compounds of chlorine, the main chemical used to kill germs and keep the pool clean. Chlorine is one of the halogens—non-metal elements in Group 7 of the Periodic Table. They are fluorine, chlorine, bromine, and iodine, all commonly used in disinfectants.

The chlorine in pool sanitizers breaks down in the water into hypochlorous acid (HOCl), a weak acid, and hypochlorite ion (ClO⁻).

Reactive Group 7

Halogen atoms only need one more electron to reach the maximum, stable number in their outer energy shells, so they are very reactive. They readily take an electron from another atom, and so become particles (ions) with a negative charge. Elements at the top of the Group are more reactive; fluorine's smaller size means the nucleus pulls more strongly on electrons of other atoms, making it the most reactive of the Group. It is one of the most reactive elements of all—it can make steel wool burst into flames.

When heated, iodine changes from the solid to a purple gas without becoming a liquid in between. This is sublimation.

HALL OF FAME:
Henry Aaron Hill
1915–1979

Hill completed his PhD at Massachusetts Institute of Technology (MIT) and later became the first Black president of the American Chemical Society. He studied compounds used to make fluorine-containing plastics. Hill established companies supplying chemicals used in plastics production, and he offered research and consultation in polymer chemistry.

DID YOU KNOW? Your body contains about 3 mg of fluoride (fluorine compounds). Fluoride guards against tooth decay, and it's added to toothpaste.

Ribbon seaweeds (kelp) take in iodine compounds from seawater, so they are a good food source. Too little iodine in the diet can cause goiter (swelling of the thyroid gland).

Hypochlorous acid and hypochlorite kill the bacteria and other microorganisms that can cause stomach and ear infections.

Chlorine compounds can irritate skin, and hypochlorite makes fabrics fade—so always rinse your body and your swimsuit when you leave the pool!

Non-stick pans are coated with PTFE (polytetrafluoroethylene), a plastic made of carbon and fluorine. When it was invented in 1938, it was the slipperiest substance known.

Poisons with Useful Compounds

The halogens are strong-smelling, poisonous elements. Their atoms can bond in pairs to form molecules with two identical atoms, but they do not exist in these pure forms in nature. They combine with other elements as compounds in rocks and the oceans. They react with metals to form ionic salts called metal halides, such as sodium chloride (table salt). The halogens behave alike, but they do not all look alike. Fluorine and chlorine are greenish gases, bromine is a dark red, oily liquid, and iodine is a black solid.

Noble Gases

The last column in the Periodic Table is Group 8. The elements in this Group are the noble gases, so-called because they won't join a gang with other atoms to make compounds. They are helium, neon, argon, krypton, xenon, and radon. They have no color or smell, and—apart from radon, which is radioactive—they are safe to use.

Inert Gases

The noble gases are known as the inert gases because they're so inactive. They don't react because they have a full outer shell of electrons. This means that they have a valency (bonding ability) of 0—they can't make bonds because they don't need to share, borrow, or lend electrons with other atoms. They exist as single atoms, but they are naturally rare—except for argon, which makes up 1 per cent of the air. We take it in with every breath, but it has no effect on our bodies.

Red neon lights contain pure neon. More "neon" colors are produced by the other noble gases. Neon lights are tubes containing the gases at low pressure.

Argon is used as a shielding gas in welding (joining metals). The equipment releases the gas around the metal as it melts, protecting it from oxygen and moisture in the air.

HALL OF FAME:
Marie Curie
1867–1934

Polish scientist Marie Curie, and her husband Pierre, discovered the elements radium and polonium from the mineral pitchblende. In 1900, they observed that radium released a gas during radioactive decay. Another scientist, Friedrich Dorn, also observed the new radioactive gas, which was later named radon. The Curies were awarded a Nobel Prize in 1903, and Marie received a second one in 1911.

Helium and Neon

Our most familiar noble gases are helium and neon. Helium, lighter than air, is used in balloons, but it's also an important cooling agent in spacecraft and advanced research equipment such as the Large Hadron Collider. Neon is used as a powerful coolant and in electrical equipment. It gives off a red glow when an electric current runs through it, and it's commonly used in advertising. The barcode scanners in stores are helium-neon gas lasers.

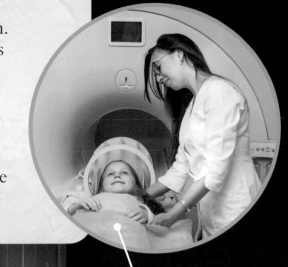

The excited electrons release energy as light. The different noble gases emit light of different wavelengths, which is why we see them as different colors.

Helium is used to cool the magnets of MRI scanners—hospital machines used for looking at details inside patients' body parts.

The gases produce the bright colors when an electric current runs through them and gives energy to the electrons in their atoms.

Old-fashioned incandescent light bulbs emit light from a heated tungsten filament. They are full of argon, which keeps the heated filament from reacting with oxygen in the air and corroding.

DID YOU KNOW? Nuclear reactors give off krypton. In the Cold War, levels of krypton-85 were used to track the secret building of nuclear weapons.

Metals

Metal elements are mainly strong, high-density, malleable (they can be shaped), and good conductors of heat and electricity, with high melting and boiling points. They usually react with oxygen to form oxides that are basic (alkaline, not acidic), and they react with acids to make a metal compound called a "salt", plus hydrogen. They lose electrons in reactions to form positive ions (cations).

Metals are good conductors of electricity because of their metallic bonds. The outer electrons are loosely bonded and can flow between the atoms, carrying the charge through the metal.

Transition and Post-transition Metals

The transition metals, which fill the central panel of the Periodic Table, are "typical" metals—hard, heavy, and shiny. They are less reactive than the highly active alkali metals and alkaline earth metals. Iron, a transition metal, is attracted to magnets. Iron alloys (mixtures) are ferrous metals and are also magnetic. The post-transition metals, or "basic" metals, include aluminum and lead. They are softer than the transition metals and have lower melting points.

Electrolysis separates metal compounds that are dissolved or molten. Here, the electric current separates copper (Cu) from copper sulfate solution.

Separating Metals

Metals occur naturally in rocks as ores— metal oxides and other compounds. They can be separated by electrolysis and other methods. Some metals, including zinc, iron, and copper, can be extracted using carbon. Carbon is a non-metal that is more reactive than those metals, so it can "displace" them—remove them from their oxides and take their place, leaving pure metal behind. That's why carbon is often included in the metals' reactivity series— the list of metals from most reactive (potassium) to least reactive (gold).

Industrial sorting claws may use magnets to separate ferrous metals such as steel from nonmagnetic materials such as aluminum and plastics.

All used metals should be recycled to avoid waste and reduce the need for mining new ores. Metals are easily recycled, but first the waste must be sorted and separated.

Alloys are often more useful than pure metals. Steel is an alloy of iron with carbon and other elements. It's stronger and lighter than iron, and is used in cars and buildings.

Stainless steel is made by adding chromium, which protects it from corrosion and rusting.

DID YOU KNOW? The metal bismuth repels magnets. So a magnet placed between an upper and lower block of bismuth will float in the air between them!

Non-metals and Semi-metals

There aren't many non-metal elements, but they are vital to life—from the carbon that builds living cells to the oxygen we breathe. Most of the Periodic Table is taken up by the metals, with the non-metals on the right of the Table. Around the zigzag line between them are the semi-metals, or "metalloids."

Semiconductors

Semi-metals—materials that sometimes conduct electricity—can be used to make semiconductors. The semi-metal silicon is like a metal because it's shiny and has a high melting point, and it's also like a non-metal because it has a low density and is brittle. It can conduct electricity in the right conditions. A pure silicon crystal can't conduct electricity because its electrons are tightly bonded. But when atoms of an impurity, such as arsenic, are added to it, an electric current can flow. This is "doping," and it allows all our electronics devices to be built around silicon.

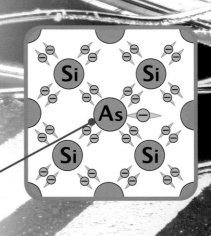

Doping silicon with arsenic gives extra, free electrons, which carry a negative charge. Doping with indium makes spaces without electrons. The spaces move as electrons flow into them, so they carry a positive charge. Both types used together make a switch.

HALL OF FAME:
Esther M. Conwell
1922–2014

Conwell was an American chemist and physicist whose love of puzzles helped her explain semiconductors. She described how electrons flow through semiconductors in the Conwell–Weisskopf theory, and the breakthrough revolutionized computing, boosting the development of everyday electronic devices. She received the Edison Medal in 1997 and the National Medal of Science in 2009.

DID YOU KNOW? In 1965, Gordon Moore correctly guessed that the number of transistors fitting on a silicon chip would double every year.

Silicon chips are inside all our electronic devices, from phones to solar panels.

"Doped" silicon is used to make electronic on/off switches called transistors, used in computers.

Thousands of transistors fit on a piece of silicon called a chip, or "integrated circuit," as small as a baby's fingernail. Tiny wires connect the components.

Microprocessors are tiny processing units etched (drawn) onto individual chips. They follow instructions and make decisions, so the computer can do its work.

The Kawah Ijen volcano in Indonesia emits sulfur that burns with a spectacular blue flame. Like other non-metals, sulfur reacts with oxygen to produce acidic oxides—in this case, sulfur dioxide.

Non-metals

The non-metal elements include hydrogen, carbon, nitrogen, oxygen, phosphorus, sulfur, and the halogens. The non-metals look and behave in many different ways, but they are all unlike metals. They don't conduct heat and electricity well; they have low melting and boiling points, as well as low densities; as solids they break easily and are often brittle, so they are not easily shaped; they are dull rather than shiny; and they are hardly magnetic at all.

Organic and Inorganic Chemicals

Atoms of carbon and hydrogen have a very important partnership. Compounds that contain carbon-hydrogen bonds are "organic," and the rest are "inorganic." Organic chemistry is all about chains of atoms—the molecules get longer as more atoms are added to the "backbone" of carbon, making series of chemicals with predictable structures and properties. The bodies of living things are made of organic chemicals that also contain other atoms, such as oxygen and nitrogen.

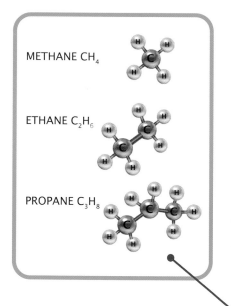

METHANE CH$_4$

ETHANE C$_2$H$_6$

PROPANE C$_3$H$_8$

Methane, ethane, and propane are the first three molecules in the alkane series. Each has one carbon and two hydrogen atoms more than the last, building up to very long chains.

Hydrocarbons

Compounds that contain only carbon and hydrogen atoms are "hydrocarbons." A carbon atom can make four bonds, and a hydrogen atom can make one bond. So, the simplest hydrocarbon is one carbon atom linked by single bonds to four hydrogen atoms—methane (CH$_4$). Methane is an "alkane," a hydrocarbon that contains no double bonds. Alkanes are good fuels; they burn in oxygen to produce carbon dioxide, water, and energy. They have predictable properties. For example, as alkane molecules get longer, their boiling points get higher.

HALL OF FAME: Saint Elmo Brady 1884–1966

Brady was the first Black American chemist to be awarded a PhD in America. He studied carboxylic acids (molecules with a special arrangement of carbon, hydrogen, and oxygen atoms) to see how changing parts of a molecule affected its acidity. He improved ways of preparing and purifying organic acids. Brady also helped develop academic facilities at Historically Black Colleges and Universities (HBCU).

DID YOU KNOW? It's estimated that an average cow releases 375 liters (82 gallons) of methane a day from both ends—the same level of pollution as a car.

A polymer molecule is a repeating structure, with molecules of the monomer linked up like beads on a chain.

Monomers

Polymerization

Polymer

Monomers and Polymers

Polymers are long, repeating chains of many small molecules called monomers. Most (but not all) polymers are organic, and some occur naturally while others are manufactured. Plastics are manufactured polymers. The strong plastic polyvinyl chloride (PVC) is a long chain of linked vinyl chloride monomers containing carbon, hydrogen, and chlorine atoms. Natural polymers include fats, starches, proteins, and wool. Nucleic acids—the molecules that carry our genetic information—are natural polymers that are particularly large and complicated molecular structures.

Plastics are organic polymers made out of chemicals from fossil fuels. Plastic bottles are made from polymers like polyethylene terephthalate (PET). They are light, bendy, and easily shaped.

Glass bottles are made from an inorganic material, silicon dioxide (SiO_2), also known as silica—or sand. It is transparent, stiff, and brittle.

Inorganic materials (like glass and metals) and organic materials (like plastics, paper, and cardboard) all should be used responsibly—reused as much as possible and then recycled.

Radioactivity

Protons are the subatomic particles that identify elements, and each element has its own number of protons. But the number of *neutrons* is different in different isotopes (forms) of an element. An isotope with more neutrons than usual is unstable and it decays (breaks up), giving off energy as radioactive particles and rays.

Half-life

When radioisotopes (unstable isotopes) break up, their nuclei give off three types of radiation: alpha particles (made of two protons plus two neutrons), beta radiation (electrons), and electromagnetic waves (gamma rays). This changes the number of subatomic particles, which means that radioactive elements change into other elements. This radioactive decay occurs atom by atom, and it happens at different rates for different radioisotopes. A radioactive isotope's "half-life" is the time it takes for half of its nuclei to decay into the atoms of another element. The half-life of radon-222 is four days.

Nuclear radiation can harm living cells—so it can also be helpful in killing germs on food and medical equipment, or killing damaged cells in cancer patients.

Plant- and animal-based pigments in prehistoric cave paintings can be dated by carbon dating. Carbon-14 can date objects up to 60,000 years old. Other radioisotopes date older fossils.

Carbon Dating

Free neutrons—not held in an atomic nucleus—occur high in the atmosphere. When one bumps into a nitrogen atom in the air, the nitrogen gains a neutron and releases a proton—and so changes into an atom of carbon-14.

Carbon-14 atoms become part of carbon dioxide molecules, and so enter the food chain through plants. Carbon-14 is weakly radioactive. All living things contain a known percentage of it, and when they die, those carbon-14 atoms decay slowly into nitrogen—the half-life is 5,700 years. How much carbon-14 is left tells us the age of long-dead things—carbon dating.

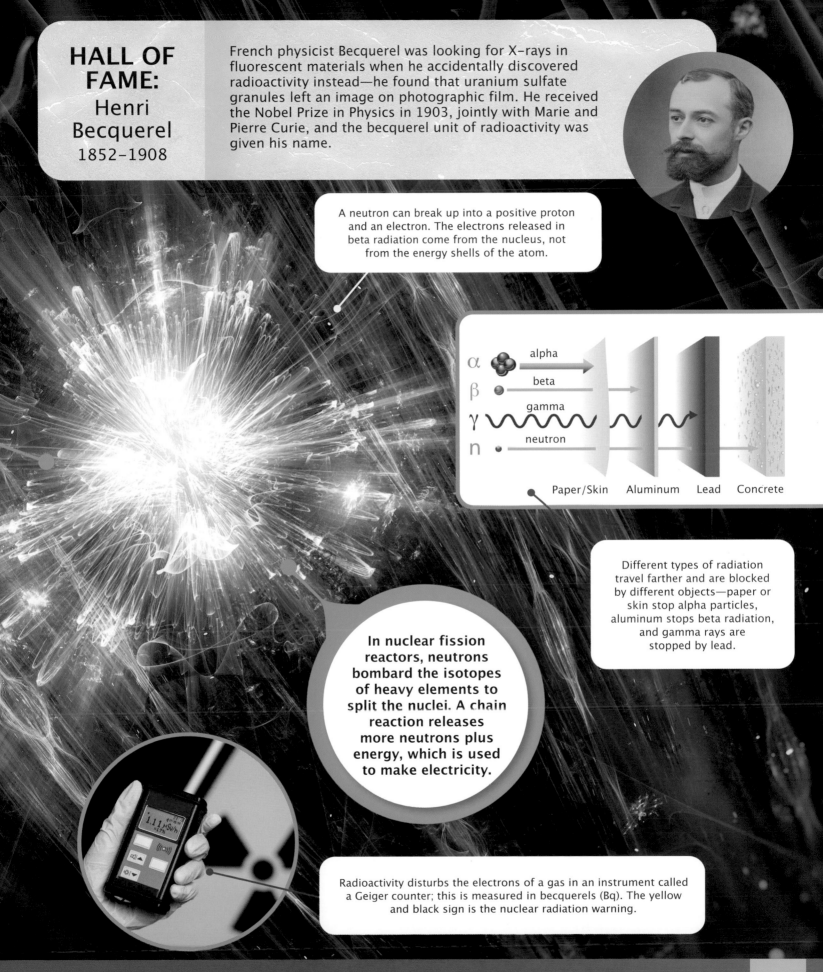

HALL OF FAME: Henri Becquerel
1852–1908

French physicist Becquerel was looking for X-rays in fluorescent materials when he accidentally discovered radioactivity instead—he found that uranium sulfate granules left an image on photographic film. He received the Nobel Prize in Physics in 1903, jointly with Marie and Pierre Curie, and the becquerel unit of radioactivity was given his name.

A neutron can break up into a positive proton and an electron. The electrons released in beta radiation come from the nucleus, not from the energy shells of the atom.

α   alpha
β   beta
γ   gamma
n   neutron

Paper/Skin   Aluminum   Lead   Concrete

Different types of radiation travel farther and are blocked by different objects—paper or skin stop alpha particles, aluminum stops beta radiation, and gamma rays are stopped by lead.

In nuclear fission reactors, neutrons bombard the isotopes of heavy elements to split the nuclei. A chain reaction releases more neutrons plus energy, which is used to make electricity.

Radioactivity disturbs the electrons of a gas in an instrument called a Geiger counter; this is measured in becquerels (Bq). The yellow and black sign is the nuclear radiation warning.

DID YOU KNOW? Earth's background radiation causes changes to genes inside cells, and so it drives natural evolution (living things developing from ancestral forms).

Chemists as Detectives

All the matter in the Universe is made of elements—the simplest chemicals. Elements combine to make compounds, and compounds get mixed up in materials. Pure chemicals contain just one element or just one compound. Chemists are detectives—they do experiments to find out what chemicals are and whether they are pure. This is "chemical analysis."

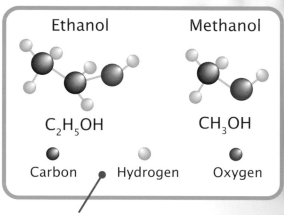

Ethanol

C_2H_5OH

Methanol

CH_3OH

Carbon   Hydrogen   Oxygen

Pure ethanol boils at 78°C (173°F), while methanol boils at 65°C (149°F). A mixture of the two boils somewhere in between.

Melting and Boiling Points

Substances change states (such as melting from solid to liquid) as temperature changes. Pure chemicals change state at known temperatures—they have their own melting points and boiling points. If other chemicals (impurities) are added to them, these melting and boiling points change. So, one way to see whether chemicals are pure is by comparing the temperatures they boil at.

Pure water freezes at 0°C (32°F). Impurities lower the freezing point, so salt sprinkled on icy roads melts the ice.

HALL OF FAME:
Marie Meurdrac
1610–1680

Meurdrac was a French alchemist who wrote *Useful and Easy Chemistry, for the Benefit of Ladies.* The book was a sign of how, in time, alchemical procedures would become modern chemistry. It contained recipes for cosmetics and medicines, and focused on low-cost treatments that could help the poor.

Experimental Procedure

Scientists follow correct procedures when they do any experiment. First, they plan the experiment and predict the results. Then they do the experiment, keeping some things the same to make sure it is a fair test. They take measurements carefully to avoid errors, and they repeat the test to make sure that the results are precise. After the experiment, they write what they found out in a conclusion.

Glass thermometers should be read at eye level, because looking at them from above or below can cause an error in the reading.

Mineral water (or tap water) is impure because other compounds are dissolved in it. The impurities make the water boil at a higher temperature.

Digital thermometers are safe to use and give accurate results.

A water molecule is a compound of one oxygen and two hydrogen atoms, chemically combined. Distilled (pure) water boils at 100°C (212°F).

DID YOU KNOW? Helium has the lowest boiling (condensation) point of all the elements. It changes from gas to liquid at a cool –269°C (–452°F).

Chromatography

Chromatography is a beautiful example of chemical analysis. It shows what's in a sample solution by separating out the different dissolved substances. It's done with a "stationary phase" (such as paper) and a "mobile phase" (a liquid to travel up the paper), and it makes amazing patterns called chromatograms.

These chromatograms were made with marker pens and strips of filter paper. They show that marker-pen inks are mixtures of different-colored inks.

Paper Chromatography

Paper chromatography uses absorbent paper to separate colored solutions. It works well for inks or dyes. Paper marked with a dot of ink is placed in a beaker of water, so the dot is above the waterline. The water travels up the paper. It reaches the dot and continues upward, carrying the ink with it. Some of the substances in the ink go farther up the paper than others, so a pattern appears above the original dot.

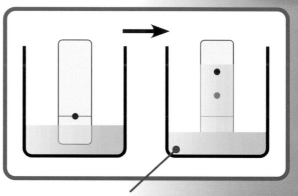

A dye with two components would make a chromatogram like this. A pure substance would make a pattern of just one color.

Gas chromatography is used to analyze urine (pee) samples from athletes, to see if they have taken banned substances to help them win.

Gas Chromatography

Gas chromatography is used to separate complex mixtures. The "mobile phase" is a carrier gas, such as helium, and the "stationary phase" is a solid, such as silica, packed into a tube or "column." The gas carries the sample, which separates into its parts as it travels along the column. A computer displays the gas chromatogram as a graph showing how many substances, and how much of them, are in the sample.

Each strip of paper was marked near one end with a pen and dipped in water, so that the water soaked up the paper. The ink components traveled with it.

Strips with the same pattern show that they were marked with the same marker ink. Can you see the two identical samples?

HALL OF FAME:
Erika Cremer
1900–1996

Cremer was a German chemist who developed the idea of gas chromatography in 1944, using a solid phase and a mobile gas phase to separate mixtures. World War II delayed publication of her work, and she was not considered for the Nobel Prize for Chemistry for the discovery, which was awarded to other scientists in 1952.

DID YOU KNOW? Chromatography has shown that people living in Peru 6,000 years ago were already making indigo dye, which is used to dye blue jeans today.

Crystals

Most solids contain a tidy arrangement of particles where the atoms, ions, or molecules are joined in regular, repeating patterns. This makes a framework called a crystal lattice, which gives the substance a certain shape. Crystals create breathtaking natural wonders, and they make chemistry great fun!

Growing Crystals

You can grow salt crystals on a string hanging in a saturated (full) solution of salt dissolved in water. The string soaks up the salt water, and the water evaporates into the air. Crystalline salt is left behind—crystals form when a dissolved solid "precipitates" in this way. Crystals also form when melted solids—like volcanic magma—cool. Diamond, for instance, is very difficult to grow in a laboratory because we need to copy the high heat and pressures found deep underground.

Hot, melted sulfur is a red liquid. As it cools, it turns into a rubbery, brown solid—and then into these yellow, "monoclinic" needle-shaped crystals.

Take a look at salt grains under a lens. You'll see cubic crystals with straight edges and right angles, because sodium and chlorine atoms link up in a square.

HALL OF FAME:
Jane Marcet
1769–1858

Marcet was an English writer who wrote educational books aimed at women. She wrote an early science textbook called *Conversations on Chemistry*, which taught chemistry through imagined talks between a teacher and her female students, after she realized that traditional public lectures were hard to grasp. Marcet's books helped to change chemistry into a more inclusive and available profession.

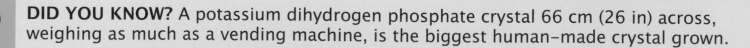

DID YOU KNOW? A potassium dihydrogen phosphate crystal 66 cm (26 in) across, weighing as much as a vending machine, is the biggest human-made crystal grown.

Heating drives the water out of blue copper sulfate, turning it white. If you add water, it changes back to blue.

Hydrated Crystals

Some crystal salts (compounds) contain "water of crystallization." These water-containing, or "hydrated," crystals seem dry, but they have water molecules trapped in their structure. Hydrated copper sulfate crystals have five water molecules attached to every molecule of copper sulfate. The chemical formula has a dot—$CuSO_4 \cdot 5H_2O$—to show this special bonding. When hydrated copper sulfate is heated, the water evaporates out of the crystal, leaving "anhydrous" (not water-containing) copper sulfate behind.

Monoclinic crystals form naturally in volcanos, but they quickly change into "orthorhombic" crystals, shaped like two little pyramids base to base.

When we melt sulfur powder in a laboratory, we see the yellow crystals form and change shape as the powder cools.

Reagents

Carbohydrates, fats, vitamins, and proteins are part of our diet, and food tests show which of them are in which foods. We can use reagents (chemicals that detect other chemicals) to do this. The tests are as simple as adding a reagent to a food sample in a test tube and observing the magical color changes.

Sudden Clouds and Disappearing Blue

Lipids are fats and oils, found in things like butter and cream. We test for them with an emulsion test—adding ethanol to a food sample in a test tube and shaking it, then pouring it into water. If lipids are present, the liquid turns cloudy. The test for vitamin C, found in fruit, is the dark blue reagent, dichlorophenolindophenol (DCPIP). The sample is added to the DCPIP drop by drop, while shaking it. If vitamin C is present, the color vanishes.

An electric water bath warms a sample to a set temperature without overheating it, but a beaker of hot water works just as well.

Changing Colors

The Benedict's and biuret reagents are both bright blue solutions. Benedict's solution tests for sugars like glucose. It's added to a sample, and the test tube is warmed gently in a water bath. The liquid changes through a series of shades if sugar is present. The biuret test is for proteins. Two reagents—copper sulfate and sodium hydroxide—are added to the food sample. If protein is present, the blue mixture turns purple.

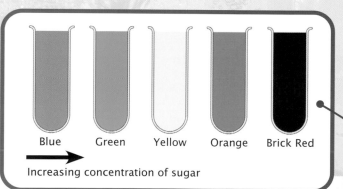

| Blue | Green | Yellow | Orange | Brick Red |

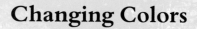

Increasing concentration of sugar

Benedict's solution turns green and then yellow or orange if sugar is present, and brick-red if there is a lot.

DID YOU KNOW? A carrot fanatic eating ten carrots every day might see their palms turn orange, due to too much of the pigment beta-carotene.

The test for starch is iodine solution, which is yellow-brown. It turns blue-black in the presence of starch.

The iodine reaction only happens with starch, so we know it's detecting starch and not sugars or other carbohydrates.

IODINE SOLUTION
0.01M

Starch is a type of carbohydrate that we need for energy. It's found in foods like bread, pasta, cereals, and potatoes.

HALL OF FAME:
Robert Boyle
1627–1691

Irish-born Boyle was the first leading scientist to carry out controlled experiments and publish the results with details about procedure, apparatus, and observation. He is most famous for Boyle's Law concerning the volume and pressure of gases, but he also introduced many standard chemical tests, including the litmus test for acids and alkalis.

Acids and Alkalis

Acids in our stomach digest our food. On the pH scale, which measures acidity and alkalinity, acids score between pH 0 and pH 6, with pH 0 being the strongest. Stomach acids score a powerful pH 1! Alkalis score between pH 8 and pH 14 on the scale. Acids and alkalis are at opposite ends of the scale, but strong solutions of both can damage materials and living tissues.

The pH scale goes from highly acidic 0 to highly alkaline 14. pH 7 is "neutral." Water is pH 7, so it's neither acid nor alkali.

Indicators

The stronger the acid, the more damage it can do. Chemists test solutions for acidity and alkalinity with "indicators." Litmus paper is dipped into a solution and shows if it is acid (by turning red) or alkaline (by turning blue). Universal indicator tells us how strongly acidic or alkaline a solution is, by changing to a range of shades. Universal indicator comes as strips of paper for dipping, or as a liquid for mixing into the test solution.

When universal indicator paper is dipped into a solution, it changes to a shade that can be matched with the pH scale.

Neutralization

Acids and alkalis neutralize each other—they react to form a salt (compound) plus water. Both the salt and the water are pH 7 (neutral). The reaction between hydrochloric acid and alkaline sodium hydroxide produces a salt called sodium chloride (table salt), but most "salts" are not table salt. The name of the salt depends on the acid that produced it. For example, the reaction between sulfuric acid and copper oxide makes copper sulfate.

Titration tests how much alkali neutralizes an acid. Alkali is added slowly, to the point where the universal indicator liquid in the mixture shows that it has become neutral.

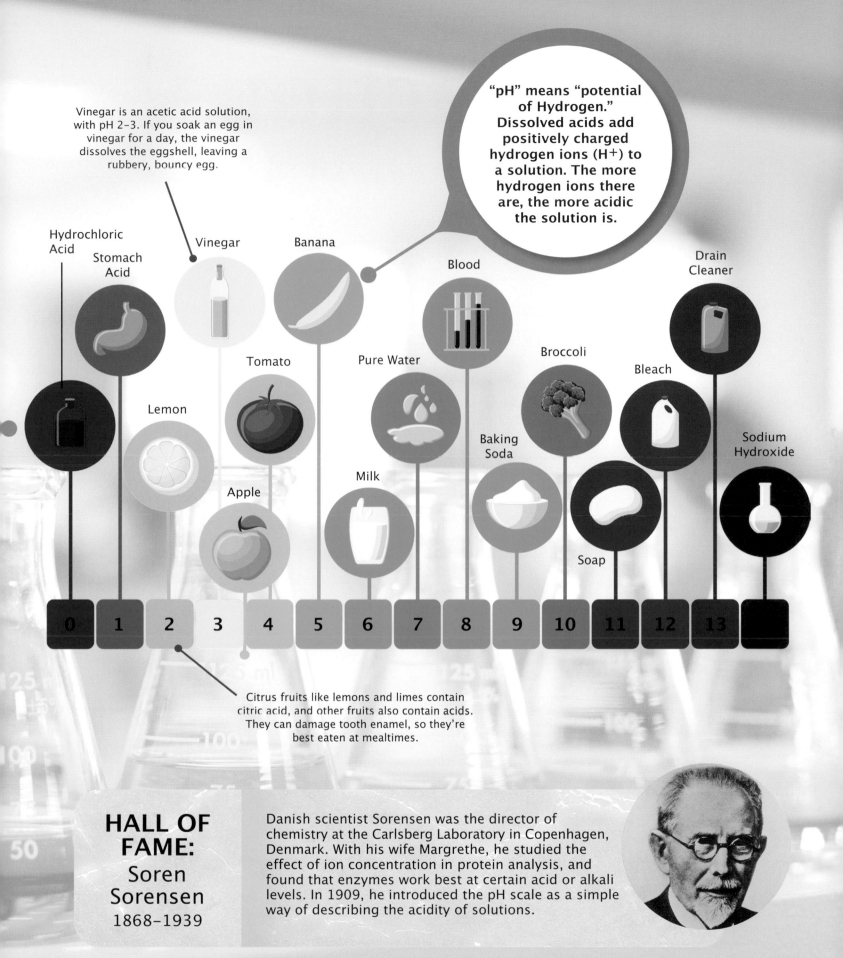

Vinegar is an acetic acid solution, with pH 2–3. If you soak an egg in vinegar for a day, the vinegar dissolves the eggshell, leaving a rubbery, bouncy egg.

"pH" means "potential of Hydrogen." Dissolved acids add positively charged hydrogen ions (H+) to a solution. The more hydrogen ions there are, the more acidic the solution is.

Hydrochloric Acid

Vinegar

Banana

Blood

Drain Cleaner

Stomach Acid

Tomato

Pure Water

Broccoli

Bleach

Lemon

Milk

Baking Soda

Sodium Hydroxide

Apple

Soap

0 1 2 3 4 5 6 7 8 9 10 11 12 13

Citrus fruits like lemons and limes contain citric acid, and other fruits also contain acids. They can damage tooth enamel, so they're best eaten at mealtimes.

HALL OF FAME:
Soren Sorensen
1868–1939

Danish scientist Sorensen was the director of chemistry at the Carlsberg Laboratory in Copenhagen, Denmark. With his wife Margrethe, he studied the effect of ion concentration in protein analysis, and found that enzymes work best at certain acid or alkali levels. In 1909, he introduced the pH scale as a simple way of describing the acidity of solutions.

DID YOU KNOW? Rainwater is naturally around pH 6, but polluted (acid) rain has been measured at pH 2. That's as acidic as lemon!

Acid Reactions

Acids are chemicals that score below 7 on the pH scale. They are corrosive—they can burn skin and damage materials, even dissolving metals—so it's very important to follow safety procedures such as wearing eye protection in laboratory experiments with acids.

Acids and Metals

Acids react with metals to make a salt (metal compound) and hydrogen. The metal displaces (takes the place of) hydrogen in the solution, and the displaced hydrogen is seen as bubbles of gas. The equation for these reactions is: acid + metal $\longrightarrow$ salt + hydrogen. For example:

sulfuric acid and zinc $\longrightarrow$ zinc sulfate and hydrogen

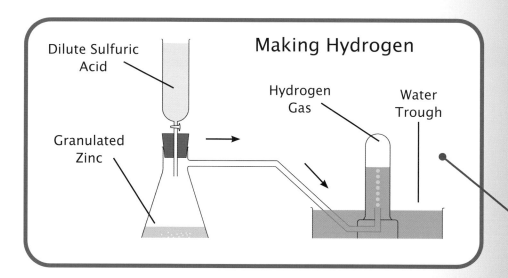

Making Hydrogen

Dilute Sulfuric Acid

Granulated Zinc

Hydrogen Gas

Water Trough

Iron is in the middle of the reactivity series—it reacts, but not violently, to dilute hydrochloric acid.

When acid and metal react in a sealed flask, hydrogen can be passed through a tube and bubbled through a water trough into a collecting tube.

HALL OF FAME:

Henry Cavendish

1731–1810

Cavendish was an extremely rich, but very shy, French physicist and chemist. He made the first attempt to calculate the weight of the Earth—with an error of only 10 per cent. He studied the properties of the gas given off when a metal and acid reacted, and so discovered hydrogen in 1766.

DID YOU KNOW? Scientists use maths and gravity to calculate that Earth weighs 6,000,000,000,000,000,000,000,000 kg (13,200,000,000,000,000,000,000,000 lb).

Holding a lit splint (a long, thin strip of wood) at the top of the tube tests for hydrogen—it will make a squeaky "pop."

Zinc sulfate is used in fertilizers and medicines, as a zinc supplement. Zinc is a trace element, needed in small amounts by all living things.

Acids and Metal Oxides

Metals react with oxygen to form oxides—compounds that contain oxygen. Metal oxides are basic (not acidic), which means they make alkaline solutions. Alkalis react with acids to neutralize each other, resulting in products of pH 7. So, the reaction of an acid with a metal oxide is a neutralization reaction, and it produces a salt plus water. For example:

sulfuric acid and zinc oxide $\longrightarrow$ zinc sulfate and water

The reactivity series lists metals from most to least reactive. The most reactive ones explode in dilute acids, while the least reactive don't react at all. Those in the middle bubble gently.

The iron nail fizzes, giving off hydrogen gas. The nail gets smaller as the reaction goes on.

Fire and Flame Tests

We can learn a lot about chemicals by burning them! Some metal salts (compounds) burn with colorful flames at very high temperatures. This happens because the salts contain positively charged ions—and different metal ions produce different flame colors.

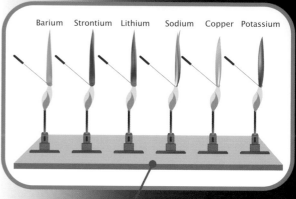

Barium   Strontium   Lithium   Sodium   Copper   Potassium

Ion identification by flame color: barium green, strontium and lithium shades of red, sodium yellow, copper blue–green, and potassium lilac.

Flame Tests for Metals

A Bunsen burner is a small laboratory gas burner. It can be adjusted to burn hotter by mixing more air with the gas as it burns. The hottest flame is "roaring blue"—a noisy, almost invisible flame. This is the flame setting used to test metals. The scientist dips a wire loop in a sample of a metal salt and then holds it in the Bunsen flame. The alkali metals—lithium, sodium, and potassium—look especially amazing in flame tests.

Splint Tests for Gases

Oxygen, hydrogen, and carbon dioxide gases are gases commonly given off, unseen, in laboratory experiments. One way to identify these invisible gases is with a lighted splint (a long, thin piece of wood). A lighted splint makes an explosive "squeaky pop" when it's inserted into a test tube full of hydrogen, and it goes out in a tube of carbon dioxide. Carbon dioxide is so nonflammable that it's used in fire extinguishers.

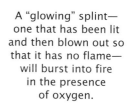

A "glowing" splint—one that has been lit and then blown out so that it has no flame—will burst into fire in the presence of oxygen.

DID YOU KNOW? A world-record firework in 2020 weighed 1,271 kg (2,797 lb) —the weight of two cows—and flew 900 m (300 ft) upward before exploding!

Fireworks contain fuel, such as charcoal, plus metals and metal salts to make the vivid colors. Oxidizing chemicals like nitrates provide oxygen to make them burn more brightly.

Blue firework colors are the hardest to produce, because the copper salts break down at very high temperatures.

Adjusting the air flow on the side of a Bunsen burner produces different flames. The hottest "roaring blue" flame is produced when the hole is fully open.

Aluminum and magnesium make bright white and silvery sparks.

Manufacturers mix different metals to get even more colors. A mixture of strontium and copper salts makes purple.

HALL OF FAME:
Li Tian
Seventh Century

In around 650 CE, a Chinese monk named Li Tian is said to have experimented with sulfur, potassium nitrate, and honey—perhaps while cooking or trying to frighten evil spirits. He stuffed the resulting mixture into bamboo shoots, which exploded in the fire, and so invented the firework. Gunpowder was probably invented later, when charcoal was added to the mix.

Electrochemistry

Electricity is an important part of chemistry. It's the result of a charge carried by particles—either electrons or ions, which are atoms that have lost or gained electrons. When charged particles flow, we get electricity, and when they flow around a circuit, we get an electric current. Some chemical reactions produce electricity, and others use electricity. This is electrochemistry.

Electrolysis

Electrolysis is splitting a compound by electricity. It needs an electrolyte (a liquid containing ions) and a positive and a negative electrode. The electrolyte may be a molten (melted) solid or a compound dissolved in water. When a current passes through it, the positive and negative ions are pulled in different directions, toward the electrodes, and the compound gets torn apart. Electrolysis of sodium chloride dissolved in water breaks the molecules into hydrogen, chlorine, and sodium hydroxide—which is used in many industries.

— Zinc   + Copper

A lemon battery works because the citric acid in the fruit acts as the electrolyte, carrying the charge between the electrodes and completing the electric circuit to light the bulb.

These steel grids are electro-galvanized with zinc to protect them against rusting.

Galvanizing

Iron and steel corrode—they react with oxygen in the air to form iron oxide, or rust, which weakens the metal. To protect them, objects made of iron or steel are "galvanized"—coated with protective zinc. Galvanizing items by "hot-dipping" them into molten zinc produces a thick, long-lasting protective coating. Galvanizing with electrolysis—electrogalvanizing—is less expensive and produces a thinner coating which is smoother and shinier but not so hard-wearing.

DID YOU KNOW? Experiments in the field of electrochemistry inspired the writer Mary Shelley to create her famous character, Frankenstein's monster.

In electroplating, metal items are coated with another metal. Here, electricity flows across a solution of silver nitrate (the electrolyte) to give a dull nickel spoon a shiny silver coat.

International Space Station astronauts don't run out of air, because electrolysis is used to split water into hydrogen and oxygen. The hydrogen is recycled back into water.

Electrochemical processes are used to process astronauts' waste products, allowing them to go on long-term Space missions.

HALL OF FAME:
Luigi Galvani
1737–1798

Galvani was an Italian scientist and doctor. Together with his wife Lucia, he noticed that electricity made the legs of dissected frogs twitch. Galvani decided that the body held "animal electricity." His ideas inspired Alessandro Volta to invent the battery, and Volta coined the term *galvanism*—meaning the production of electricity by chemical reaction—out of respect for Galvani.

Spectra

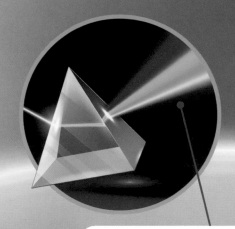

There's a rainbow inside sunlight. The colors are mixed up, so it looks colorless—"white light." Light energy travels in waves. When we see different colored light, we're seeing waves of different lengths—blue light has shorter waves than red light.

When light passes through transparent objects like raindrops or a prism, the wavelengths bend and spread into a rainbow, which is one type of spectrum.

Absorption and Emission Spectra

Atoms absorb and emit specific colors of light. Very hot objects, such as stars, produce white light. When this white light shines through a cold gas, the elements in the gas absorb some of the colors. This creates an absorption spectrum with dark stripes where light has been removed. The colors of the missing light tells us what elements are in the cloud. A cloud of hot gas produces a few colors of light. This is the emission spectrum, and the colors also show what gas is in the cloud.

This pattern of stripes in the absorption and emission spectra is like a fingerprint saying, "Oxygen was here!"

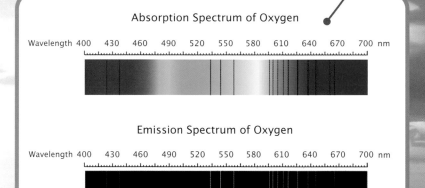

Absorption Spectrum of Oxygen

Wavelength 400 430 460 490 520 550 580 610 640 670 700 nm

Emission Spectrum of Oxygen

Wavelength 400 430 460 490 520 550 580 610 640 670 700 nm

HALL OF FAME:
Alma Levant Hayden
1927–1967

Hayden was a Black American chemist. She was an expert in spectrometry and led the team that analyzed Krebiozen. This expensive chemical was sold as a "wonder drug" for treating cancer, but Hayden showed it was a useless fake. Hayden became head of the spectrophotometer research branch of the Pharmaceutical Chemistry Division of the FDA in 1963.

Objects reflect (bounce back) wavelengths of their own color, and they absorb (soak up) other shades of light. Leaves look green because they reflect green light and absorb the rest.

In a double rainbow, the colors in the higher rainbow are reversed!

When sunlight passes through raindrops in the sky, the light splits to form a visible light spectrum—a rainbow.

When sunlight hits Earth's atmosphere, the short waves of blue light are scattered more than the other colors, and so we see a blue sky.

Mass Spectrum

A mass spectrometer is a racetrack inside a magnetic field. Ions (charged particles) from a chemical sample race along a tube, and the magnetic field deflects them—it makes them move in a curve. How much they curve depends on their mass. Lighter ions deflect more than heavier ones. The ions are detected at the end of the tube, and the results appear as a graph—a "mass spectrum" showing which elements are present and how much.

This mass spectrometer analyzes chemicals in a medical laboratory. The sample is vaporized and ionized at the front of the instrument.

DID YOU KNOW? The longest–lived rainbow ever recorded occurred in 2017. It lasted for 8 hours and 58 minutes!

Seeing Atoms and Molecules

A light microscope can magnify objects as tiny as 300 nanometers—that's 200 times smaller than the width of a hair. This magnification is helpful, but it will never let us see atoms or molecules. Scientists need much more powerful instruments to do that.

This image of atoms in a crystal magnified 100 million times was taken by scientists using electron ptychography at Cornell University. It was published in 2021.

Microscopes

Transmission electron microscopes use a beam of electrons. Electrons have a much shorter wavelength than visible light, so an electron microscope is 250 times more powerful than a light microscope. A technique called electron ptychography has made the resolution (detail) better, producing amazing 3D images of atoms inside crystals. Scanning probe microscopes give a computerized view of atoms by using a tiny probe—only an atom wide itself—like a tiny finger which "feels" atoms and the spaces between them.

X-Ray Crystallography

When electromagnetic waves, such as light waves or X-rays, travel through small spaces, they diffract (scatter). This means that when X-rays shine through a crystal, they spread out as they pass between the atoms, making a pattern. With the help of computers, analysts use the X-ray patterns to map the positions of the atoms and make 3D models of the molecules.

In 1953, an X-ray diffraction image like this gave scientists the clue that the structure of a DNA molecule was two strands in a spiral structure—a double helix.

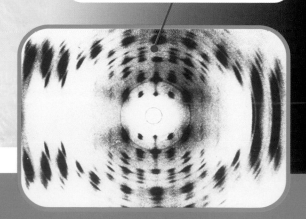

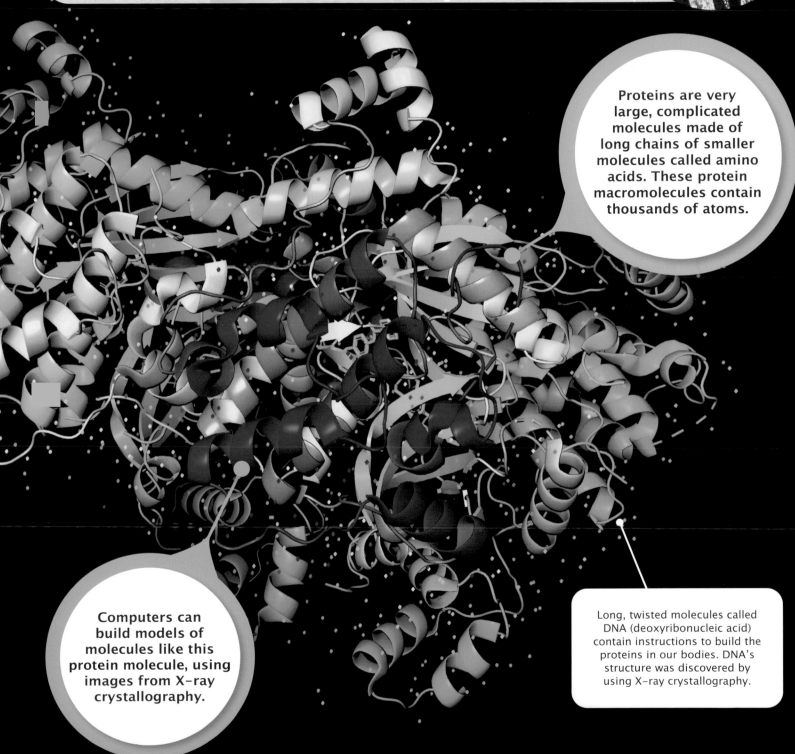

Proteins are very large, complicated molecules made of long chains of smaller molecules called amino acids. These protein macromolecules contain thousands of atoms.

Computers can build models of molecules like this protein molecule, using images from X-ray crystallography.

Long, twisted molecules called DNA (deoxyribonucleic acid) contain instructions to build the proteins in our bodies. DNA's structure was discovered by using X-ray crystallography.

DID YOU KNOW? The largest protein in your body is titin. One molecule has a mass of 3 million, and its chemical name is so long, it takes three hours to say!

The First Chemistry

It is thought that 13.8 billion years ago there was nothing but a tiny area, so full of energy that it burst in a huge, hot explosion. This is the Big Bang theory. It explains how the Universe began and how it's still expanding. The theory is supported by the elements that we can detect out in space, across the Universe.

Star Birth

Absorption spectra—the "fingerprints" of elements—show that 99.9 per cent of our Sun is hydrogen and helium, with tiny amounts of other elements. Other stars are the same. Hydrogen and helium are the lightest atoms, and they formed first after the Big Bang, making gas clouds. The clouds collapsed to make protostars—balls of hot gas containing the charged particles, electrons, and hydrogen ions. Nuclear fusion began to "burn" hydrogen ions, joining the nuclei to make helium and the first starlight.

The Forging of Elements

Nuclear fusion deep in the Sun's core turns hydrogen into helium, and produces energy. As any star ages, its core runs out of hydrogen fuel and starts fusing helium instead. When helium fuel runs out, the nuclei of larger atoms start to fuse and produce the heavier elements, up to iron. When the star's core runs out of fuel, it collapses. In the case of giant stars, huge energies then produce the heaviest elements, and scatter them in a supernova explosion.

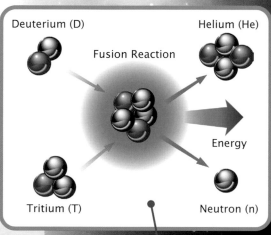

The nuclei of hydrogen isotopes deuterium and tritium have one positively charged proton (red). They fuse to make a helium nucleus with two protons. More nuclei additions make heavier elements.

DID YOU KNOW? New stars burst into life by starting nuclear fusion at temperatures above 15,000,000°C (27,000,032°F).

British–American astronomer and astrophysicist Payne–Gaposchkin studied at Cambridge University, UK, but, as a woman, received no degree. She became the first woman to earn an astronomy PhD from Radcliffe College, USA, and was a trailblazer for women. She saw that the Sun's spectrum had far more hydrogen and helium than other elements, and realized that hydrogen was the most abundant element in the stars.

The Horsehead Nebula is 1,600 light-years away—its light takes 1,600 years to reach Earth.

Galaxies are groups of stars. They also contain gas and dust clouds—nebulae—where stars are born. The Horsehead Nebula looks like a chess piece.

The Orion star constellation is like a dot-to-dot of a hunter with his bow. Find the star called Alnitak at the bottom of his belt to look toward the Horsehead Nebula.

The stars are chemical factories. Except for hydrogen and helium and a few others, all the elements' atoms in the Universe were made inside stars.

You are star stuff—you are made of atoms that were built in the stars billions of years ago!

Our World

Our Solar System formed 4.6 billion years ago, from a cloud of dust and gas around the Sun. Near the hot center, dust gathered into rocks, and rocks collided and clumped together, eventually forming Earth. The molten materials inside the planet arranged themselves into layers—heavier elements sank to form the core, and lighter materials floated upward, cooled, and hardened.

Young Earth

As Earth cooled, blocks of rock floating on molten rock became the crust. Volcanic gases erupted and began to form the atmosphere. When Earth had cooled to below the boiling point of water, water in the atmosphere condensed and began a rainstorm that lasted for centuries. Water gathered in hollows on the surface and made the first oceans. Today, the Earth's crust is still active and changing. It moves in huge "tectonic plates" and recycles itself through volcanic activity.

As the Moon orbits Earth, its gravity pulls on the oceans, making tides which help life thrive. Tides also drive the ocean currents, helping to keep Earth's climate stable.

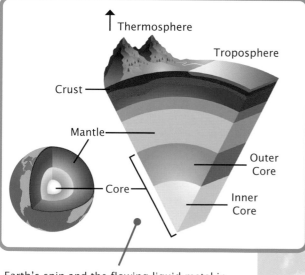

Thermosphere

Troposphere

Crust

Mantle

Outer Core

Core

Inner Core

Earth's spin and the flowing liquid metal in the outer core put a magnetic field around the planet, which protects our atmosphere from solar winds and radiation from Space.

Layers of Earth

Earth has a heart of iron and nickel—a solid inner core surrounded by a liquid outer core. The layer above the core is the mantle, made of hot, slowly flowing, semi-molten rock, or magma. The crust is the outer layer of solid rock, where we live and oceans flow. Surrounding it all are the gases of the atmosphere. The atmospheric layer where we breathe air and where aircraft fly is the troposphere. The International Space Station is in the thermosphere.

DID YOU KNOW? The pale patches on the Moon's surface are anorthosite—a type of rock also found on Earth—suggesting that the Moon was once part of Earth.

On dark nights, we can see the galaxy stretching, like a highway across the sky. Our Sun is one of hundreds of billions of stars in the Milky Way galaxy.

Earth formed with just the right amounts of elements to make a rocky surface and the hot metallic core.

The young Earth had all the chemicals—such as carbon, oxygen, and hydrogen—needed to make the molecules of life, plus the Sun's energy to support life.

Earth circles the Sun in the "Goldilocks Zone"—the perfect distance where the temperature is just right for water to exist as liquid.

HALL OF FAME:
Florence Bascom
1862–1945

Bascom was the second US woman to earn a geology PhD, having been segregated from male classmates at Johns Hopkins University. She was the first woman to work for the US Geological Survey, and she founded the geology department of Bryn Mawr College, helping to train other women. Bascom was an expert in minerals and crystals, and she discovered that rocks that were previously thought to come from sediments from lava flows.

Rocks and Minerals

Around 150 million years ago, this rock would have been a huge sand dune. Over time, winds blew the sand into layers of different grain sizes.

Earth's crust is in the recycling business. Elements and compounds combine into minerals, which are mixed up in rocks. Over thousands of years, rocks are taken underground and back up to the surface by movements of the crust and volcanic activity.

Rocks lifted to the surface are weathered and eroded, and the cycle goes on.

The Rock Cycle

Rocks get broken and worn down—eroded—by forces like the weather. Rivers carry the small pieces to the sea where they are laid down as sediment. The weight of sediment layers squashes them, forming "sedimentary rocks." Rocks buried very deep, with high temperatures and pressures, change into "metamorphic rocks," such as marble. When metamorphic rocks are heated until they melt, the molten rock—magma—comes to the surface in volcanoes, and cools as "igneous rocks," such as granite.

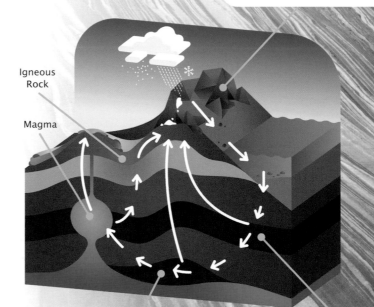

Igneous Rock

Magma

Metamorphic Rock

Sedimentary Rock

HALL OF FAME:
Marie le Jars de Gournay
1565–1645

Gournay was the adopted daughter of the French philosopher Michel de Montaigne. As a writer and early feminist, she argued for gender equality, insisting that women had the same rights as men to education and in the workplace. She performed practical experiments using alchemy, mineralogy, and philosophy, defining herself as an educated individual in a male-dominated society.

Rock Minerals

There are thousands of minerals, but only about 200 are common in rocks. Sedimentary rocks are often mainly one mineral. For example, limestone is made from seashells, so it's mostly calcium carbonate. It forms the metamorphic rock marble, so marble is also mainly calcium carbonate. Sandstone is made from compacted sand, which is silica, or silicon dioxide—a compound of silicon and oxygen, the two most common elements in Earth's crust. Heat and pressure turn sandstone into the metamorphic rock, quartzite.

The sandstone has been shaped by rain and wind. The weathering reveals the strata— the uncountable lines and ridges of the formation.

Pumice is foamed, igneous rock. It erupted from a volcano like fizzy pop from a shaken bottle, then cooled quickly, with holes where the gas bubbles had been.

The Wave is a sandstone formation in northern Arizona, USA. The rock is unusual because it formed in the desert, not under the sea.

Eventually, the sand compacted into stone. The colors are due to iron, manganese, and other mineral salts in water seeping through the porous sandstone.

DID YOU KNOW? Earth's oldest rocks are igneous "faux amphibolites" in Canada. At 4.28 billion years old, they were probably once part of Earth's earliest crust.

91

Wonderful Water

Water is Earth's superpower! Our planet is just the right distance from the Sun for liquid water to exist. Without water, life on Earth could not happen, because biochemical reactions happen in water inside living cells. Luckily, Earth recycles our precious water.

Water molecules freeze into six-sided crystals. The six arms of a snow crystal are built up from a tiny, six-sided plate of frozen water vapor.

The Water Cycle

A puddle dries up, but the water isn't lost. Water evaporates— the Sun's heat constantly turns molecules at the surface of seas, lakes, and rivers into water vapor in the air. The vapor rises, cools, and condenses into droplets inside clouds. The droplets get heavier, until they fall as raindrops or snow— precipitation. Rain falling on land flows into rivers or seeps through rocks and eventually collects in the sea. Evaporation returns water to the air, and the cycle continues.

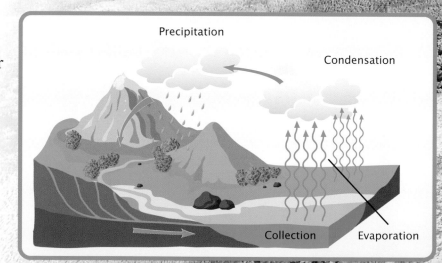

Precipitation

Condensation

Collection

Evaporation

HALL OF FAME:
Chandrasekhara Venkata Raman
1888–1970

Raman was an Indian physicist who won the Nobel Prize in physics in 1930, for his work in spectroscopy and the scattering of light. He described water as "the elixir of life" after standing on the edge of the desert beside the Nile valley in Egypt and seeing the difference between the empty desert sand and the fertile land by the river, where life thrived.

The River Danube splits to form a fan-shaped area of swampy land along the coastline—a delta. This river mouth in Romania is one of three main channels.

An estuary is where a river meets the sea. The fresh water of the river mingles with the seawater, so estuaries have "brackish" water that's slightly salty.

Sediments carried by the river are deposited in deltas and estuaries. The rich soils and the actions of the tides form unique ecosystems and wildlife habitats.

The River Danube begins in Germany and touches ten countries on its 2,850-km (1,770-mile) journey to the coast of the Black Sea.

Pond skaters can walk on water because water molecules stick together. This "cohesion" makes surface tension, which the insect is too light to break through.

The Very Odd Molecule

Water is a compound of hydrogen and oxygen—atoms so light that water should be a gas at room temperature, but it's a liquid. When it freezes, we'd expect it to become denser, but it expands. So solid water—ice—floats instead of sinking, which means icebergs insulate the sea underneath and help to keep Earth cool. Water molecules are "sticky," so trees can draw water up against gravity, to their topmost leaves. Water is a truly surprising substance!

DID YOU KNOW? There could be life on Mars! Water once flowed on the planet's surface, and scientists think there's still liquid water underground.

Creative Carbon

Carbon is the basis of the chemicals of life. It can make anything from a microbe to a whale because of the way its atoms bond (join up) with each other and with other atoms, especially hydrogen, oxygen, and nitrogen. The carbon acts like a backbone, stringing all these atoms together into long, strong molecules that make the carbohydrates, proteins, and fats that build living things.

Chemical Factories

Plants are natural factories. They absorb carbon dioxide (a compound of carbon and oxygen) from the air and use it, with water, to make glucose (a sugar) and oxygen. This is photosynthesis. In turn, the glucose molecules make bigger carbohydrates that build the plant's body.

You are a chemical factory, too! When you eat a plant or an animal in the food chain, you use its carbon and other atoms to make proteins that build your own body. This happens in nearly all your body cells—the chemical instructions are kept in long molecules called DNA, packed into every cell.

Photosynthesis makes glucose, a molecule with six oxygen and 12 hydrogen atoms on a chain of six carbon atoms. Glucose makes bigger molecules that build living things.

Coal, gas, and oil are the remains of plants and animals that died millions of years ago. Burning these fossil fuels releases carbon dioxide into the atmosphere.

The Carbon Cycle

Living things return their carbon atoms to the environment in different ways. Carbon dioxide is made during respiration (a process that releases energy), and it leaves your body when you breathe out. Carbon is also given out in waste, like fallen leaves or our poop, and the bodies of dead plants and animals. Organisms in the soil, called decomposers, help this waste break down into simple chemicals that plants can absorb. The decomposers release carbon dioxide into the air during respiration. Plants take the carbon dioxide to make sugars, and the carbon cycle goes on.

In 1634, Belgian chemist van Helmont planted a young willow tree in a pot of soil. After five years, the tree was 30 times heavier, but the soil's weight had hardly changed. This experiment showed that the plant was getting nutrients from somewhere other than the soil, and it helped later scientists to discover photosynthesis.

Think of trees and people as a team! Trees make oxygen for us to breathe, and we make carbon dioxide for them to use in photosynthesis.

When trees photosynthesize, they lock carbon into their bodies. This helps reduce carbon dioxide in the atmosphere, and that helps control global warming.

Plants contain chlorophyll, a green pigment that absorbs energy from sunlight. They use the energy to power photosynthesis.

DID YOU KNOW? More than half of your body weight is water—and if you take away the water, half of what's left is carbon!

Essential Oxygen

Many living things need oxygen for respiration—the process of getting energy from glucose. Oxygen gas makes up around 21 per cent of Earth's atmosphere. Like other chemicals widely used in biological processes, it's never used up, but keeps being recycled through the environment.

The Element

Oxygen is the third most abundant element in the Universe, after hydrogen and helium. It's the most common element in Earth's crust, making up 47 per cent, mostly combined with silicon. It's also the most common element in your body, mainly inside water. Pure oxygen has no color, smell, or taste. It reacts readily with other elements to make compounds called oxides. Oxides are everywhere— water is an oxide of hydrogen, sand is an oxide of silicon, and rust is an oxide of iron.

Oxidation is the addition of oxygen atoms to chemicals. An apple goes brown after it's cut and exposed to air, because of an oxidation reaction.

Many land animals breathe air and oxygen into their lungs, but a fish gets oxygen by taking water into its mouth and passing it over feathery gills in its head.

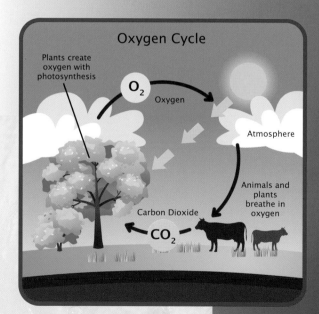

Oxygen Cycle

Plants create oxygen with photosynthesis

O_2 Oxygen

Atmosphere

Animals and plants breathe in oxygen

Carbon Dioxide

CO_2

The Oxygen Cycle

Plants on land and sea drive the oxygen cycle by photosynthesis—they use the Sun's energy to turn carbon dioxide and water into glucose and oxygen. The oxygen is released to the air, and plants and animals use it for respiration. Respiration is the opposite of photosynthesis—it turns glucose and oxygen into carbon dioxide and water. At the same time, energy is released which the animal or plant uses for chemical reactions in its cells.

DID YOU KNOW? Giant dragonflies lived 300 million years ago, when higher oxygen levels meant that their tiny breathing tubes could get more oxygen.

Oxygen moves from the seawater into blood vessels in the gills, and it's carried by the blood to the fish's body cells, where respiration happens.

Tiny sea-living organisms called cyanobacteria started to produce oxygen by photosynthesis about 2.5 billion years ago, and so began to add oxygen to Earth's atmosphere.

Respiration with oxygen is "aerobic." "Anaerobic" respiration—without oxygen—can also happen, for example, in our muscle cells during heavy exercise.

HALL OF FAME:
Joseph Priestley
1733–1804

Carl Wilhelm Scheele produced oxygen in Sweden in 1771, but did not publish his discovery until six years later. Meanwhile, English scientist Joseph Priestley published his discovery of oxygen in 1774, after collecting the gas that was produced from mercuric oxide heated by the Sun. Priestley found that the gas made breathing easier and made a candle burn more brightly.

Team Nitrogen

Nitrogen makes up most of Earth's atmosphere. Living things need it to make proteins, but there's a problem. Nitrogen atoms in the air bond strongly in pairs, and the bonds must be broken before the nitrogen atoms can form other compounds. Luckily a team of soil bacteria and plants called legumes (peas and clover) can help.

Nitrogen atoms can make three bonds, so two atoms link up with very strong triple bonds, making an unreactive molecule of the diatomic element N_2.

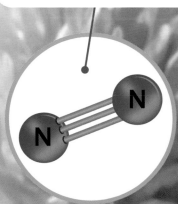

The Nitrogen Cycle

Helped by plants like clover, "nitrogen-fixing" bacteria recycle nitrogen in the environment. The bacteria "fix" nitrogen—they separate the N_2 atoms so they can combine in compounds called nitrates. The nitrates are absorbed by plants and used to make proteins. Nitrogen atoms pass through the food chain until they return to the soil in plant and animal waste or dead bodies. Then different bacteria recycle them into either nitrates in the soil or pure nitrogen in the air.

Lightning, volcanoes, and fire also "fix" nitrogen by breaking apart the N_2 molecules, allowing the free nitrogen atoms to combine with other elements.

Haber Process

The Haber process is an industrial method that fixes nitrogen by turning nitrogen gas and hydrogen into ammonia (NH_3). The ammonia is made into nitrogen-based fertilizers like ammonium nitrate, which help farm crops grow. However, overuse of fertilizers can put too much nitrate into rivers and streams, and upset the nitrogen cycle. Alternative methods of adding nitrates to soils are crop rotation with legumes, and the use of natural fertilizers like manure (poop).

DID YOU KNOW? Early Egyptian alchemists made "sal ammonia" (ammonium chloride) for smelling salts by heating dung (poop) and urine (pee) with salt.

Some nitrates in the soil are converted back into N_2 in the air by "denitrifying bacteria."

Farmers enrich their fields by planting fields of clover. Nitrogen-fixing bacteria in the clover roots turn nitrogen from the air into nitrates.

The bacteria form nodules on the clover roots, where nitrates build up. The clover uses the nitrates, and animals that eat the clover gain the nitrogen.

Decomposers—tiny organisms in the soil—and "nitrifying bacteria" break down the waste from living and dead animals and plants, making more nitrates available.

Crucial Glucose

Every living thing is building up and breaking down molecules all the time. All these chemical reactions together are its metabolism. Glucose is particularly important in metabolism. It's a monosaccharide—a simple sugar made of just one molecule.

Getting Glucose

Plants make glucose from carbon dioxide and water, with energy from the Sun. They use the glucose to make bigger molecules, like cellulose and starch. Plants are the producers in the food chain, and we are the consumers—we get glucose from plants when we eat starchy foods like bread, rice, and potatoes. Digestion breaks the starches down into simple sugars, which our blood carries to our tissues. There, tiny cell structures release energy from the molecules, for use in cell processes.

Green parts of plants absorb sunlight and trap the energy in glucose molecules during photosynthesis. Energy is stored in the bonds between atoms inside the molecules.

The formula of a glucose molecule is $C_6H_{12}O_6$ because it has six carbon atoms, with 12 hydrogen atoms and six oxygen atoms attached.

Making Polysaccharides

Monosaccharides join up in chains to make long natural polymers called polysaccharides. Glucose molecules ($C_6H_{12}O_6$) link up to make polysaccharides, like starch and cellulose. As each glucose molecule links up, a water molecule (H_2O) is lost, so the polysaccharide formula is ($C_6H_{10}O_5$)n, where n means any number of repeated molecules. Starch is an untidy molecule, used to store energy. Cellulose is a straight molecule, used to build strong structures like tree trunks.

DID YOU KNOW? The human brain accounts for around 2 per cent of body weight, but uses around 20 per cent of the glucose energy needed by the body.

Plants can't live around deep–sea hydrothermal vents with no light. Instead, the food chain producers are bacteria, making glucose from hydrogen sulfide and methane by chemosynthesis.

Glucose is stored as starch in leaves, stems, roots, and seeds—or in fruit, like pumpkins. The energy-giving, digestible nutrients we get from starchy foods are carbohydrates.

Glucose is carried from the leaves to the plant's cells. It is used either to release energy during respiration, or stored, or used to make larger molecules to grow the plant's body.

HALL OF FAME:
Marie Maynard Daly
1921–2003

Daly was the first Black woman to earn a PhD in chemistry in the United States. Her studies focused on the role of enzymes in starch digestion, and on the structure and biochemical activities of the cell nucleus. Daly taught biochemistry and became a professor at the Albert Einstein College of Medicine. She also pushed to enroll more minority students in medical and scientific studies.

Plant Chemicals

Plants and fungi don't seem to do much, but in fact they're busy doing amazing chemistry! There are chemical reactions going on in their bodies all the time—their metabolism. A plant has the important "job" of trapping energy and making glucose to build its body—but the chemicals of photosynthesis aren't the only ones involved in its everyday life.

Plant Hormones

Plants need light, and they can seek it out. They have hormones (chemical messengers) called auxins that control the growth of their root and shoot tips. Auxin in a shoot tip moves away from light. It concentrates in the shadiest side of the shoot and makes the cells there grow faster—so the shoot bends toward the light. Auxin in a root tip diffuses downward in response to gravity. It makes the cells grow slower on the underside of the tip, so the root grows down.

Many plants contain poisonous chemicals that taste bad, to discourage munching. Ragwort (*Senecio*) is a British wildflower that contains toxic chemicals called alkaloids.

Most of a fungus's body is hidden underground. Fungi aren't plants, so they don't photosynthesize. They break down decaying material to get to the nutrients inside.

Wood Wide Web

Trees look solitary, but they share food and chemical messages as a community. Hyphae—threads of fungi—link the tree roots underground, making a network called the "Wood Wide Web." The fungi get glucose from the trees and give nutrients in return, and they make a pathway for trees to share stuff. Older trees feed sugars to seedlings, while less friendly trees send harmful chemicals. Plants also know when other plants close to them are being eaten, and respond by making protective chemicals in their own leaves.

DID YOU KNOW? The Venus flytrap can count! When an insect touches its sensory hairs, the plant counts two touches before snapping the trap shut.

The black and yellow markings of this type of caterpillar, and the red and black markings of the adult moth, warn predators that they taste bad—so they are less likely to get eaten!

Cinnabar moth caterpillars feed on ragwort. The plant's toxins don't hurt them, but stay in the caterpillars' bodies, making them poisonous too.

Ragwort can harm farm animals if they eat a lot of it, but it supplies nectar and pollen to many insects, and it's important for biodiversity.

Tree leaves contain red and yellow pigments, which act as sunscreen. They're hidden by the green pigment chlorophyll, so we see them in the fall, when trees stop producing chlorophyll.

Body Chemistry

Out of all the millions of chemicals, just a few organic (carbon-based) compounds are used by living organisms. These "biomolecules" include proteins, carbohydrates, lipids, and nucleic acids. Animal bodies are built from these molecules, and the chemical reactions that involve them are their metabolism.

Social insects like ants live and work together in a colony. They communicate with chemical signals—pheromones—that carry messages to all the members of the colony.

Proteins

Proteins are polymers (long-chain molecules) made of building blocks called amino acids. There are around 20,000 different proteins in your body, including hemoglobin, which carries oxygen in red blood cells. Your muscles work because proteins contract and slide over each other. Enzymes that break down your food are proteins, and so are hormones—chemical messengers like adrenaline and insulin. Nucleic acids, found in chromosomes, are not proteins, but they are the chemicals that carry the code to make proteins.

Skeletons

Skeletons are hard structures that protect animals' soft tissues, hold them up, and help them move. Animals with backbones have a bony, inner skeleton made of a protein called collagen, strengthened with calcium phosphate. Many invertebrates have skeletons outside their bodies—an insect's exoskeleton is like a suit of armor made of a polymer called chitin, while snails and other mollusks build shells out of calcium carbonate.

Jellyfish are 95 per cent water! Even their skeletons are made of water. The water pressure gives their bodies shape, and they squirt it out one way to move in the opposite direction.

DID YOU KNOW? Your smile shows off the hardest compound in your body—tooth enamel. It's made of a calcium phosphate crystal called hydroxyapatite.

DNA

Adenine

Thymine

Cytosine

Guanine

Phosphate Backbone

The nucleic acid DNA carries the code for making proteins in a long chain of four compounds—adenine, thymine, cytosine, and guanine. The code is passed on to offspring.

The ant colony is like a "superorganism," with individual ants acting like cells, organized and working together inside one creature.

When an ant finds food, it leads the others to it with a trail of pheromones. If food is too heavy for one ant to lift, a group carry it back to the colony as a team.

Ants use pheromones to warn each other of danger. And the queen ant's pheromones tell her daughters she is laying eggs, so they don't have to.

HALL OF FAME:
Lloyd Noel Ferguson
1918–2011

Ferguson grew up during the depression. He became the first Black American to earn a PhD in chemistry from the University of California, USA, and in 1958 he started up the first PhD program in chemistry at a historically Black college. His research studies included the structure and biological activity of carbon-based molecules, and the differences between sweet- and sour-tasting molecules.

Food Chemicals

Like all animals, we must build and repair our bodies to stay healthy. To do that, we need biomolecules—but we can't use sunlight to make these chemicals like plants do. Instead, we eat plants, or animals that eat the plants.

People with type 2 diabetes follow a careful diet to keep their blood sugar (glucose) steady. They may take insulin to control their levels.

Nutrients

A human may have 37 trillion body cells, and every minute about 300 million of them die and are renewed. The nutrients we need to do all that building are found in different food groups, so we need to combine those foods for a balanced diet. Fresh, raw foods are good for us, because nutrients are lost during processing and cooking. But some foods, like meat, must be cooked to kill germs, improve taste, and help us digest them.

An enzyme in your saliva breaks down starch into sugars. Keep on chewing bread, and it will start to taste sweet.

We need starchy foods like bread, pasta, and cereals for carbohydrates, to give us energy, fiber, calcium, and vitamins. Sugary foods are less healthy carbohydrates than starchy foods.

Additives

Many foods are "fortified" to replace nutrients lost in preparation, or to add extra nutrients. Vegans don't get Vitamin B12 from plants, so it's added to soy-based foods. Other additives make foods last longer on the shelf, or add color, taste, or texture. Additives may be natural, like plant extracts, or human-made, like the sugar substitute, saccharin. In Europe, food additives are given E numbers to show that they have been tested and found safe. Food labels list E numbers among all the other ingredients.

Curcumin (from turmeric) is a health food and colorant. It has carbon, hydrogen, and oxygen atoms in the formula $C_{21}H_{20}O_6$ and its E number is E100.

DID YOU KNOW? Pufferfish contains tetrodotoxin—a deadly poison. Chefs train for years and take an exam before they are allowed to cook and serve it.

HALL OF FAME:
Norbert Rillieux
1806–1894

Rillieux, one-quarter Black, was born free on a New Orleans plantation and became a pioneer chemical engineer. He produced sugar from cane juice by repeated evaporation at reduced pressures, and so invented the multiple effect evaporator to produce better-quality crystals at a lower cost. This less dangerous production process revolutionized the sugar industry.

A third of our diet should be fruit and vegetables. They give us vitamins for healthy cells, fiber to help move food through our gut, and also water—but we still need to drink lots of it.

For proteins, we need fish, meat, and eggs, or vegetable proteins like nuts, beans, and pulses (dry seeds), so we can build and repair our bodies.

Milk, cheese, and butter give us oils and fats for energy. Dairy products and meat supply minerals like iron for healthy cells.

Cleaning Chemicals

A lot of washing goes on in our homes. Good hygiene means cleaning ourselves, our clothes, and all our things. Oddly, water isn't very good at cleaning. Luckily, chemistry can help. There are some truly cool chemicals in your bathroom!

Plain soaps are practical, but dyes and other additives may be used to give them interesting colors, scents, and textures.

Cleaning and Disinfecting

Water molecules like their own company—surface tension makes them stick together, so they stick less to surfaces and dirt. Soaps and other detergents help because they are surface-acting agents—"surfactants." They reduce the surface tension of water so it can stick to dirt on other surfaces. Some household cleaning products contain disinfectants to kill germs and sterilize surfaces. Bleach, a whitening agent that removes stains and kills germs, is a solution of chemicals including sodium hypochlorite (NaOCl).

How Soap Works

A soap molecule has two halves and a dual nature. It has a soluble, hydrophilic "head" that's attracted to water, and a hydrophobic "tail" that hates water but loves the fats and oils in dirt. The hydrophilic end dissolves in the water in the washing solution, while the hydrophobic part dissolves in the dirt—this means that the soap molecule lets water grip the dirt. As we scrub the soap into our skin and hair, the soap molecules lift the dirt and break it up into small structures called "micelles" suspended in the water, ready to be rinsed away.

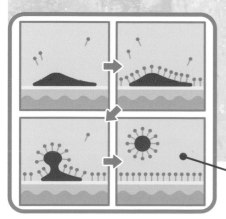

When the soap molecules surround the micelles, the water-loving ends of the soap molecules point out to the water, and the water-hating ends point in to the dirt.

DID YOU KNOW? Soap has been made for 2,000 years. Pot ash was made by seeping wood ash in water, which then reacts with fat to make soap.

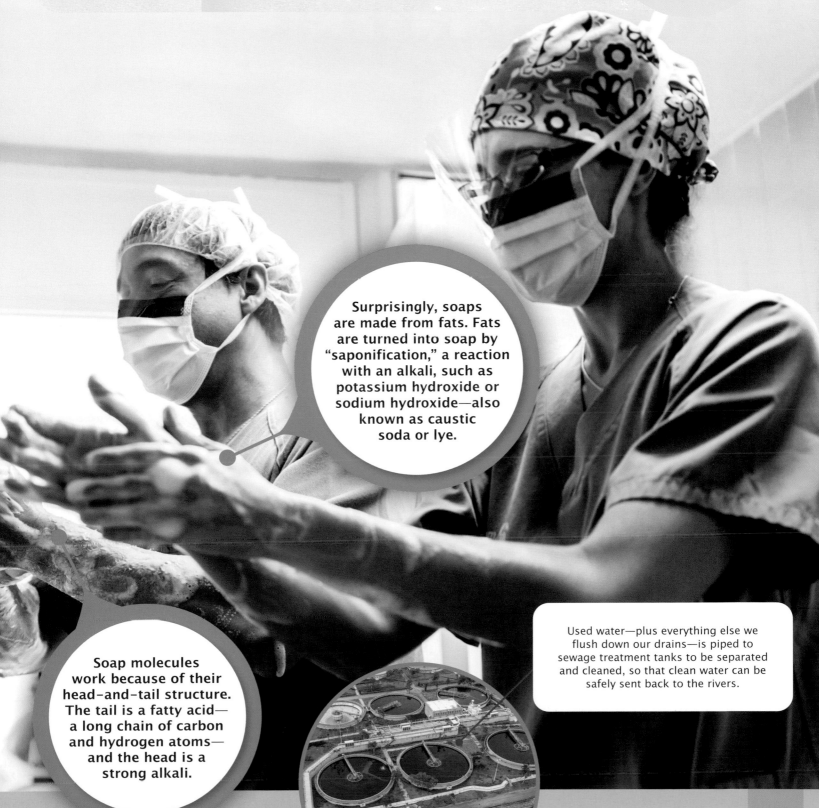

Hall was a Black American inventor who held 59 US patents on preserving food, including a way to cure meats by combining salt with other sodium salts. He realized that some spices introduced germs and made food go bad. He found a way to sterilize the spices with ethylene gas in a vacuum chamber, and the idea was later used by the food, drug, and cosmetics industries.

Surprisingly, soaps are made from fats. Fats are turned into soap by "saponification," a reaction with an alkali, such as potassium hydroxide or sodium hydroxide—also known as caustic soda or lye.

Soap molecules work because of their head-and-tail structure. The tail is a fatty acid— a long chain of carbon and hydrogen atoms— and the head is a strong alkali.

Used water—plus everything else we flush down our drains—is piped to sewage treatment tanks to be separated and cleaned, so that clean water can be safely sent back to the rivers.

Chemistry at the Pharmacy

Medicines help us get better when we're sick. But the wrong medicine, or too much of it, can also make us ill. Pharmacists are trained chemists and health care professionals. They prepare the drugs that doctors prescribe, and give advice about over-the-counter drugs (medicines sold without a doctor's prescription).

Antibiotics kill bacteria (germs) which can cause infections. Doctors only prescribe them when necessary, because some germs are changing so that the drugs no longer work. This is antibiotic resistance.

Development of Medicines

Ancient people discovered herbal remedies when they noticed that eating certain plants made them feel better. Many of our drugs originally come from natural sources—aspirin is based on salicylic acid from willow bark, while penicillin was discovered in a mold called penicillium. Modern drugs are carefully tested to make sure they are effective, safe, and given in the right amounts.

Most medicines now are made by pharmaceutical companies, which means they can be produced in large quantities and—importantly—in clean, safe laboratories.

HALL OF FAME:
Percy Lavon Julian
1899–1975

Julian was a Black American chemist and director of chemicals development at the Glidden Company. His research included producing versions of plant compounds called steroids in the laboratory in large amounts for use in medicines. He made physostigmine for treating eye disease, and he developed large-scale production of cortisone drugs and the hormones progesterone and testosterone.

Companies give their medicines different brand names, such as "Calpol" and "Tylenol"—the names of paracetamol syrups sold to treat fever and pain.

Over-the-counter drugs treat minor problems, such as coughs, colds, allergies, and skin disorders. The pharmacy also sells vitamins and food supplements, as well as supplying the medicines that doctors prescribe.

Vaccines

Most people get vaccinated against things like measles, mumps, and rubella as children, and get more vaccines as adults. Vaccines protect us against infectious diseases by mimicking the virus or other bug, so the body's immune system is ready to fight when it meets the real infection. Normally it takes 5–15 years to develop a vaccine. During the COVID-19 pandemic, international scientists worked together and mapped the chemical sequence in the new virus's DNA in just ten days!

The COVID-19 virus is one of many coronaviruses. Scientists' knowledge of the make up of other viruses helped them to develop a COVID-19 vaccine in just one year.

Various pills are made to be swallowed, chewed, or dissolved in water. Capsules have a coating that dissolves in the stomach to release the medicine.

DID YOU KNOW? A snake's venom can contain over 100 compounds. Scientists use some to treat disorders of the heart, kidneys, blood clotting, pain, and cancer.

Soil and Agrochemicals

Soil feeds and supports plants. It's made of tiny particles from weathered rocks mixed up with humus (organic matter from living things). Sandy soil has large particles and drains quickly, while clay soil has small, sticky particles that hold water. Farmers use fertilizers and other agrochemicals to help their food crops grow.

Cutting down forests or overgrazing land causes soil erosion—soil is worn, blown, or washed away, leaving depleted land where crops grow poorly.

Fertilizers

Healthy plants take the right amounts of minerals and other nutrients from the soil. As each crop is harvested, the nutrients are used up—the soil becomes "depleted." Farmers replace the nutrients with fertilizers such as nitrogen and NPK (nitrogen, phosphorus, and potassium). These release nutrients quickly, but they are easily washed away into rivers, where they can poison the water.

Monoculture needs agrochemicals, because the single-crop plants have the same genes, so are easily attacked by pests and disease.

Pesticides

A problem with growing food is that other creatures may get there first! Farmers wage war on insects like sap-sucking aphids, leaf-chomping caterpillars, and stem-burrowing beetles, as well as slugs, snails, and worms. They also battle diseases, like fungi, and other plants (weeds). Insecticides, herbicides, and fungicides are pesticides—agrochemicals used to tackle these problems. Pesticides are effective, but they can harm other living things and disturb ecosystems.

DID YOU KNOW? "Organic" means compounds with carbon-hydrogen bonds, but in common use, "organic food" is food grown without human-made chemicals.

"Organic" farmers may replace soil nitrogen by adding manure (poop) and compost (decaying vegetation) instead of synthetic (human-made) fertilizers.

In-field flower strips are wild flowers planted in strips between crops. The flowers feed helpful insects like wasps, whose larvae eat pests.

Natural fertilizers are broken down by soil bacteria, so they release nutrient nitrates slowly. Large amounts are needed to keep nutrient levels high.

HALL OF FAME:
George Washington Carver
1864–1943

Carver was born into slavery months before it was banned. He studied botany at Iowa State Agricultural College and was the first Black American to earn a BSc degree. He ran the agricultural school at Tuskegee Institute, and he realized that overused cotton fields could be restored by crop rotation with nitrogen-fixing plants like peanuts. He also developed many uses for peanuts!

Classroom Chemistry

Science lessons are a good place to learn about chemistry. But every other lesson, from algebra to art, depends on chemicals, too! Everything in nature and everything anyone has ever invented or discovered is made of chemicals.

If you're lucky, your science teacher might demonstrate the endothermic chemical reactions that change cake mixture into cupcakes.

Calculators

It's best not to take your calculator apart, but if you did, you'd find a small battery, a rubber membrane, a touch-sensitive circuit, and a processing chip. Pressing one of the plastic buttons squashes the rubber membrane underneath. This makes an electrical contact that's detected by the processing chip, which uses transistors—tiny, electronic on/off switches—to do the calculations. The liquid crystals in the LCD (Liquid Crystal Display) contain molecules lined up like those in a solid crystal, but which flow and change shape like a fluid.

Glitter is made of aluminum and polyethylene terephthalate (PET), and causes microplastics pollution. Cellulose-based alternatives may be better, or you can make your own from salt and food dye.

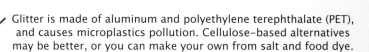

Adhesives

Adhesives are used everywhere, in many forms. Sticky notes became a sensation after scientists discovered that tiny glue bubbles called microspheres stuck lightly to surfaces and came off again. Glue sticks are nontoxic, washable glues that are based on a water-soluble polymer called polyvinylpyrrolidone (PVP), or sometimes a more environmentally friendly starch-based adhesive. PVA glue is a solution of polyvinyl acetate, which dries into a strong glue as the water evaporates after application. Epoxy glue is an epoxide resin which sets when it's mixed with a hardener.

Paper clips are usually made from galvanized (zinc-coated) steel wire, often with bright plastic coatings.

Colored pencils contain a mixture of pigments, minerals, binding agents, and resins or waxes. The wax is a delivery agent —it rubs off on paper, taking the pigment with it.

Marker pen inks are made from dyes or pigments, solvent, and stabilizing polymers to stop them clotting. Blue and black fountain pen ink is based on iron salts like ferrous sulfate.

Paper is made from wood chips, pulped in acid, bleached, flattened, and dried. Erasers are made of a rubbery material mixed with an abrasive such as pumice.

HALL OF FAME:
Ida Freund
1863–1914

Austrian-born Freund was the first female university chemistry lecturer in the UK. For classroom fun, she once made a Periodic Table out of frosted cupcakes, chocolate, and candies. She ran summer schools to help her students improve their science teaching skills. She published two chemistry textbooks and campaigned for the Chemical Society to admit women. Despite a disability, she kept up her cycling hobby, using an adapted, arm-powered tricycle.

DID YOU KNOW? Chinese court official Cai Lun first made paper sheets from wood fiber in around 105 CE, after watching wasps chew wood to make nests.

Plastics

Plastics are polymers. Their molecules are long chains of small molecules (monomers) repeated like beads on a necklace, and many monomers link up or "polymerize" to make the polymer. Polymer molecules have a "backbone" of linked carbon atoms, with atoms of other elements branching off them. Examples of polymers are polystyrene, polyethylene, and PVC.

Products made of natural polymers like corn starch are biodegradable and can be recycled into fertilizers—but they must be disposed of carefully.

Versatile but Problematic

Plastics are tough, light, waterproof, and flexible. They can be film, sheet, or foam, and they're made into all sorts of objects, such as bottles and medical equipment. They are everywhere, and that's a problem. Waste plastics hang around for decades or centuries, sometimes breaking down in the oceans into pieces smaller than 5 mm (0.2 in) long. These tiny, harmful microplastics can be swallowed by sea creatures and carry toxins into the food chain. Burning plastics releases climate-changing carbon dioxide. And plastics are nonrenewable—the fossil fuels they come from are running out.

Polymerization

The monomer vinyl chloride (VC) is a gas that polymerizes to make the strong plastic polyvinyl chloride (PVC), which is made into pipes. The secret of how a monomer like VC polymerizes is the double bond between its carbon atoms. This double bond can break to make single bonds. This means the two carbon atoms remain joined by a single bond, but each of them can also link up with a carbon atom in another VC molecule. This happens many times, joining any number of VC molecules into a chain—a PVC molecule.

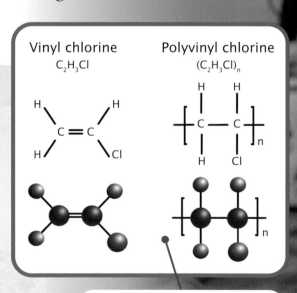

Vinyl chlorine
C_2H_3Cl

Polyvinyl chlorine
$(C_2H_3Cl)_n$

Vinyl chloride has just six carbon, hydrogen, and chlorine atoms in its molecule—the formula is C_2H_3Cl. The formula of the polymer PVC is $(C_2H_3Cl)_n$ where n can be any number of C_2H_3Cl molecules in the chain.

HALL OF FAME:
Alexander Parkes
1813–1890

The first manufactured plastic was invented as an alternative to ivory and tortoishell when demand began driving elephants and turtles toward extinction. British chemist Parkes made cellulose nitrate by dissolving cotton fiber in acid and mixing it with vegetable oil, and he patented it as "Parkesine" in 1862. It was later developed into celluloid, which made everyday items like hair combs cheaper and available to more people.

Even recyclable plastics can only be recycled once or twice before they degrade too much to be useful. In the end, they cause pollution, just like "single-use" plastics.

Scientists are racing to develop alternatives to plastics, as well as looking for ways to break down existing waste plastics into reusable chemicals.

The Global Ecobrick Alliance, which started in the Philippines, turns waste plastics into ecobricks—bottles stuffed with other waste plastics for use in buildings.

Everybody can help fight the plastics crisis by following the "reduce, reuse, recycle" rule. But recycling alone can't solve the problem. We all need to become less dependent on plastics.

DID YOU KNOW? Every minute, around one million plastic drink bottles are sold around the world—and over 40 per cent of plastic is thrown away after one use.

Clothing Chemicals

Clothes are important. They keep us warm, but we also wear them for fun and to show our personalities. Textiles are fabrics based on fibers and threads that might be woven, knitted, or felted. Turning them into clothing involves some chemicals, and has an effect on the environment.

Elastane (spandex) is a stretchy synthetic fiber used in sports clothes. The latest technology allows the textile to adjust the fit and strength of its grip, like a second skin, as the wearer moves.

Synthetic Materials

Human-made fibers, such as nylon, polyesters, and acrylates, are polymers made from chemicals extracted from fossil fuels. Like other plastics, they are not sustainable—fossil fuels will run out—and they don't decompose, so they cause pollution. Scientists are looking for better, more environmentally friendly ways to produce and recycle polymers.

We can make nylon in a school laboratory by mixing its monomers in a flask. Long nylon polymers form, making a thread-like strand.

HALL OF FAME: Stephanie Louise Kwolek 1923–2014

Kwolek was an American chemist who researched synthetic polymers and fibers for the DuPont company. She developed a flame-resistant polyamide fiber, sold as Nomex, and she also invented industrial fibers including Kevlar, a material five times stronger than steel, used in bulletproof vests, spacecraft, and many other products.

Many synthetic fabrics are cheap to produce and cheap to buy, so they are often quickly thrown away—this is the polluting downside of "fast fashion."

Natural Fibers

Wool, cotton, and silk are natural polymers—long molecules with repeating units. Cotton is made of plant cellulose, while wool and silk are animal proteins. They are renewable, sustainable, and biodegradable, but even natural fibers must be processed. Growing cotton takes lots of water, and dyeing it also uses water and can cause pollution. Wool fibers contain fats and dirt that are removed with detergents and other chemicals before dyeing. Try repairing, sharing, or donating your old clothes before throwing them away!

Silk threads come from silk moth caterpillar cocoons. Cellulose from plants like lotus and bamboo can make a vegan alternative.

Engineers at MIT (Massachusetts Institute of Technology) developed a polyethylene fiber that draws sweat away from the body. The technology could be used to recycle plastic bags into sports fabrics.

The fashion industry has a huge environmental footprint—it produces 10 per cent of global carbon dioxide emissions.

DID YOU KNOW? It can take up to 10,000 liters (2,200 gallons) of water to make just one pair of cotton jeans!

Construction Chemicals

Materials such as cement, bricks, asphalt, metals, wood, coatings, glass, and gypsum are used in construction, from bridges to roads and skyscrapers. Construction chemicals include adhesives, sealants, coatings, insulation materials, composites, and concrete admixtures.

Concrete and Cement

We see gray, stone-like concrete in buildings everywhere. Concrete is an "aggregate"—crushed rock—and is prepared with a cement paste. Cement is made from minerals like limestone and contains calcium, silicon, aluminum, and iron. It's mixed with water to make the paste, which coats the concrete aggregate and acts as a binding agent. Newly mixed concrete can be formed into shapes, and it hardens to be strong and long-lasting. Admixtures are other ingredients added to improve concrete, such as SBR (styrene butadiene rubber).

Road-building asphalt is a mixture of aggregates and a liquid binding agent called bitumen—a thick, sticky substance produced from crude oil.

Composites

Composites combine two or more materials into a substance that's more useful than the starting materials. For example, steel reinforcing bars (rebars) give concrete extra strength and flexibility. "Nanocomposites" contain nanomaterials—tiny materials measured in nanometers (billionths of a metre). The nanomaterial graphene is a single layer of graphite just one carbon atom—or 0.345 nm—thick. Newly developed nanocomposite coatings made of lime with graphene can help keep temperatures stable inside buildings, so saving energy.

The Sydney Opera House is built from steel-reinforced concrete.

DID YOU KNOW? The Three Gorges Dam in China is made of 28 million cubic meters (37 million cubic yards) of concrete, which took 17 years to pour!

Insulating materials in walls and ceilings keep the building warm and save energy by stopping the heat from leaking outside.

Waterborne coatings don't contain dangerous solvents. To make them even more environmentally friendly, manufacturers are trying to reduce other ingredients like surfactants.

An eco-friendly house may have walls insulated with layers of wood and plant cellulose. Other types of insulation are inorganic fibers and plastic foam.

Solvent-based paints contain solvents made from crude oil, and may release volatile organic compounds (VOCs), causing air pollution.

HALL OF FAME:
Edgar Purnell Hooley
1860–1942

Tarmac, or "tarmacadam,"—a material used for road surfacing in the UK—is named after John McAdam, who first made roads from crushed stone in 1820. But Welsh surveyor Hooley added tar to the mix and so invented a smooth road surface. He had the idea after noticing that an area where gravel had been dumped over an accidental tar spill had solidified into a smooth, dust-free surface.

Chemicals in Cars

Most cars are run on gasoline or "gas" (petrol) or diesel fuels, made from crude oil. These fossil fuels are finite, which means they will run out, and we can't replace them. Also, burning them produces climate-changing carbon dioxide and pollutants. Scientists are developing clean, sustainable alternatives, like biofuels, hydrogen fuel, and electric vehicles.

Gasoline (Petrol)

Crude oil is made of hydrocarbons—molecules of carbon and hydrogen—of different lengths. The shorter-chain molecules are volatile (have a low boiling point), and they are needed to make gas (petrol). Oil refiners can make more of the short hydrocarbons by "cracking" (breaking) longer molecules. This is sometimes done with catalysts—"catalytic cracking." The shorter molecules in the oil are separated out by boiling at different temperatures (fractional distillation), then blended with other liquids to make a fuel mixture suitable for car engines that burn fuel by spark plug ignition.

Diesel fuel is made from less volatile, longer-chain hydrocarbons than gasoline (petrol). It's cheaper to produce, and more efficient—but it produces more carbon dioxide, sulfur, and other pollutants.

HALL OF FAME:
Gertrud Johanna Woker
1878–1968

The Swiss biochemist and pacifist Woker studied and taught at Bern University. She warned of the dangers of leaded gasoline (petrol) and condemned poison gas, germ warfare, and atomic weapons. Books she wrote were burned by the Nazis. She experienced much sexism in her career and was denied the title of professor for over 20 years, but she is now recognized as one of the most influential women in chemistry at that time.

DID YOU KNOW? It would take the materials in 300 smartphone batteries to build a single electric car battery.

Pistons inside the engine cylinders move down to take fuel vapor and air into the combustion chamber. Then the intake valve closes, and the piston moves up, compressing the gas.

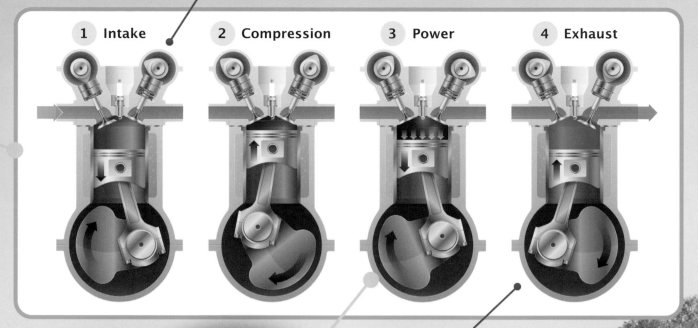

1 Intake **2** Compression **3** Power **4** Exhaust

The car engine's piston movements cause spark plugs to fire under pressure, igniting the fuel. Fuel can ignite too soon—"antiknock" additives like MMT help it ignite at the right pressure.

The turning crankshaft converts the heat into mechanical energy. The combusted gases and pollutants leave the car through the exhaust pipe, then the cycle begins again.

Biofuels and Electric Vehicles

Biofuels are renewable fuels produced from organic waste and crops like soybeans. Biofuels emit fewer polluting emissions—but crops grown for fuels may destroy land for food crops and rain forests. Electric vehicles, which use lithium-ion batteries, are clean to run, but the batteries are charged with electricity from fossil fuels. Also, battery recycling methods must be perfected to recover their precious metals—lithium, cobalt, nickel, and others.

Computer software can 3D-print car parts by depositing layers of melted plastics or metals. One day, this could make cars lighter and less environmentally damaging.

Household Energy

Most of our household energy comes from the Sun. Other sources are geothermal energy, where underground hot water and steam generate electricity, and nuclear energy, where uranium and plutonium atoms are split to release energy stored inside their nuclei.

Researchers in Cambridge, UK, have designed ultra-thin artificial leaves that turn sunlight and water into clean fuel as efficiently as plants. These flexible devices could one day create floating solar farms.

The Sun's Energy

Plants trap the Sun's energy by photosynthesis. We can use that stored chemical energy by burning fuel, whether it's fossil fuels (the remains of long-dead organisms) or biomass, like wood or kitchen waste. We can also harness the Sun's energy through wind, wave, and tidal power, and solar cells. Generating electricity from any energy source has some disadvantages, and scientists worldwide are meeting the challenges with amazing technological advances.

A hydroelectric facility pumps water uphill into a reservoir. When released, the stored water flows downhill, turning a turbine to generate electricity.

Nonrenewable and Renewable Resources

Nonrenewable energy is energy taken from resources we can't replace. There will be no new fossil fuels once existing crude oil, natural gas, and coal are gone. Renewable energy comes from resources that don't run out, or else they can be replaced. Energy stores that can be used without being depleted (used up) are "sustainable." Power plants currently use a mixture of fossil fuels, renewable resources, and nuclear power to generate electricity. As society moves toward clean, sustainable energy, everyone can help by saving energy wherever we can.

DID YOU KNOW? All our power, worldwide, could come from renewable energy resources by 2050—if governments and societies make the right decisions.

Brand was a German chemist who longed to find the fabled "philosopher's stone" which alchemists thought could turn cheap metals into gold. He thought human urine was the key, and collected all his friends' pee to help his search He didn't find what he wanted, but he did become the first person to discover an element—he found a white material in the pee, and he called it phosphorus because it glowed in the dark.

Constant motion of the ocean waves and tides drives turbines to generate electricity. The energy is renewable, clean, and reliable—but dams and barrages can harm existing ecosystems.

Sunlight will never run out. Solar panels contain photovoltaic (PV) cells that generate renewable electricity from sunlight. One day, new technology may mean we could turn entire rooftops into giant solar cells.

We burn wood, crops, and waste organic materials to generate electricity. Biofuels and biomass are sustainable, but farming biofuels can destroy ecosystems or food-crop farmland.

The wind will always blow. Wind turbines turn their blades to face the wind, capturing kinetic (motion) energy, which is converted into electricity and fed into the national power grid.

Glossary

ACID
A chemical with a value lower than 7 on the pH scale.

ALCHEMIST
An early scientist who hoped to change substances such as ordinary metals into gold.

ALKALI
A solution with a value higher than 7 on the pH scale. Alkalis neutralize acids, producing a chemical salt.

ALLOY
A mixture of a metal with a different element, often another metal.

ATOM
The smallest unit of a chemical element.

ATOMIC NUMBER
The number of protons in an atom. An element's atomic number decides its position on the Periodic Table.

CARBOHYDRATES
A group of organic chemicals including sugars and starches.

CHEMICAL BOND
A force that holds atoms together. Chemical bonds are made by sharing electrons (covalent bond) or by losing or gaining electrons (ionic bond).

CHEMICAL REACTION
A process in which atoms are rearranged, changing one or more substances into different substances.

CHLOROPHYLL
A green pigment in plants that absorbs light and turns it into chemical energy via photosynthesis.

CLIMATE CHANGE
A gradual change in Earth's average global temperature. Scientists believe that human activity is causing rapid global warming.

COMPOUND
A pure chemical made from the atoms of more than one element.

CONDUCTOR
A material that lets heat or electricity pass through it.

CRYSTAL
A solid material where the particles are joined together in a repeating pattern.

DENSITY
The space a substance takes up (its volume) in relation to the amount of matter in the substance (its mass). If a substance is small but heavy, it has high density.

DISSOLVE
When a solid is mixed with a liquid and it seems to disappear, it has dissolved.

DISTILLATION
A process where a mixture made up of liquids with different boiling points can be separated.

DNA
Deoxyribonucleic acid, a long molecule found in the cells that carries instructions for the structure and function of living things.

ELECTRON
A negatively charged particle found in an atom.

ELEMENT
A chemical made of a single type of atom. Elements are the simplest chemicals.

FILTERING
Separating solid particles from a fluid (liquid or gas).

FORMULA
The way scientists write down symbols to show the number and type of atoms present in a molecule.

FOSSIL FUELS
Coal, crude oil, and natural gas. They are nonrenewable energy sources that add to climate change.

GRAVITY
A force of attraction that exists between any two masses.

HORMONE
A chemical that controls bodily processes such as growth.

INSULATOR
A material that heat or electricity cannot pass through.

ION
An atom that carries an electric charge because it has lost or gained an electron. A cation is a positive ion, and an anion is a negative ion.

ISOTOPES
Forms of an element where the atoms have the same number of electrons and protons, but different numbers of neutrons.

MATERIAL
What a substance is made of, for example, ceramic, metal, or plastic.

MATTER
What everything in the Universe is made of. All matter is made up of tiny particles called atoms.

MINERAL
Naturally occurring inorganic solid with a defined chemical structure.

MOLECULE
A group of two or more atoms that are chemically bonded. The smallest unit of a pure substance that has the chemical properties of the substance.

MONOMER
A small molecule that links up with others like it to form a larger molecule called a polymer.

NANOMATERIAL
A material no more than 100 nm (0.0001 mm) long or wide. Particles this small are "nanoparticles."

NEUTRON
A particle found in the nucleus of an atom. Neutrons have no charge (neither positive nor negative).

NUCLEUS
The center of an atom. The plural is nuclei.

ORBITAL
An energy shell around the nucleus of an atom, where electrons move around in a wave.

ORGANIC CHEMICALS
Carbon-based compounds. Living bodies are built from organic chemicals.

OXIDATION
A reaction in which a chemical gains oxygen atoms. The substance that gains oxygen is said to be oxidized.

PERIODIC TABLE
The system used to arrange chemical elements by their atomic number.

pH
Almost all liquids are either acids or alkalis, on a pH scale of 0–14. From 0–7 are acids; from 7–14 are alkalis. Neutral substances such as pure water are 7 on the scale.

PHOTOSYNTHESIS
A process that uses water, carbon dioxide, and energy from sunlight to produce food for plants in the form of glucose.

POLYMER
A very large, chain-like molecule made of repeated smaller molecules.

PROTON
A positively charged particle found in the nucleus (center) of an atom.

RADIOACTIVE
A radioactive element gives off radiation—small particles of energy.

REACTIVITY
A measure of how easily a substance reacts with other substances.

RESPIRATION
The process living things use to release energy, involving a chemical reaction that uses glucose.

SEMICONDUCTOR
A material that lets electricity pass through it under some conditions.

SOLUBLE
Describes a material that dissolves in water. Something that won't dissolve is "insoluble."

SOLUTION
Created when a substance dissolves in a liquid.

SPECTROSCOPE
An instrument used to separate and study the wavelengths of light.

STATES OF MATTER
Solid, liquid, or gas. Matter takes a different state, depending on how its molecules are arranged.

SUBATOMIC PARTICLES
Particles inside an atom, including electrons, protons, and neutrons.

VIRUS
A tiny organism that reproduces inside living cells, often causing illness.

Index